MW01235131

My Favorite Recipes

Compiled by
Helen J. Moncrief

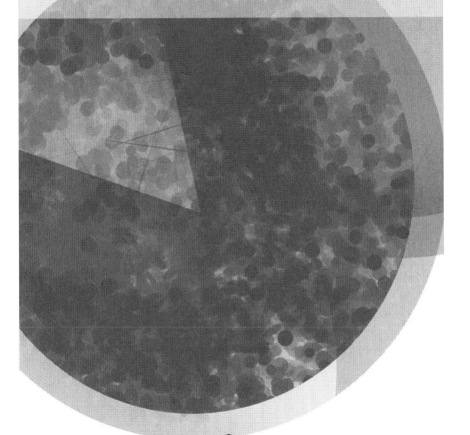

Bloomington, IN   Milton Keynes, UK
authorHOUSE®

AuthorHouse™
1663 Liberty Drive, Suite 200
Bloomington, IN 47403
www.authorhouse.com
Phone: 1-800-839-8640

AuthorHouse™ UK Ltd.
500 Avebury Boulevard
Central Milton Keynes, MK9 2BE
www.authorhouse.co.uk
Phone: 08001974150

First published by AuthorHouse 12/14/2006

ISBN: 978-1-4259-5628-8 (sc)

Library of Congress Control Number: 2006907214

Printed in the United States of America
Bloomington, Indiana

This book is printed on acid-free paper.

MY FAVORITE RECIPES

After over 50 years of marriage, raising two children and
Retirement I finally found time to gather my favorite recipes.
More than 150 lavishly recipes result in marvelous, vividly favored
foods. The idea started when I decided to compile recipes for my
daughters for their Christmas presents. Many of their friends and
family loved the recipe book, so I decided to have it published.

In these pages you'll find quick meals but, if you have the itch to cook Something from scratch, there are recipes for that, too. The recipes reflect my style of life, which is tightly interwoven into the context of my family Life as well as countless gathering with friends.

My mother was a great cook! "Mama" worked all week, therefore, she would cook enough food on the weekend for the entire week. By Sunday afternoon, a galaxy of divine flavors - Fried chicken, hearty main dishes, potato salad, collard or turnips greens, slivers of red peppers, black - eye peas and the freshness of garlic floated throughout the house. This was coupled with the aroma of freshly baked buttery rolls, blackberry, peach or cherry Cobbler and luscious sweet-potato pie.

Some of the recipes were gathered from many corner of America. Many kinds of soups, appetizers, beverages, breads, cakes, desserts, fish, steak, pork chops, and tacos. All kinds of pies, salads and vegetables. Quickly made sauces, barbecue chicken and ribs, and marinades add instant hits of flavor with little effort. enjoy!

MY FAVORITE RECIPES

COMPILED BY HELEN J. MONCRIEF

PASTA, RICE AND GRAINS

PIES

POULTRY

SALADS

SOUPS & SAUCES

VEGETABLES

APPETIZERS&
SNACKS

BARBECUE-STYLE CHICKEN WINGS

1 1/2 POUNDS CHICKEN WINGS (ABOUT 8)

1/2 CUP OPEN PIT BARBECUE SAUCE

1/4 CUP FINELY CHOPPED ONION

1 TABLESPOON HONEY OR SUGAR

1 TABLESPOON VINEGAR

1 CLOVE GARLIC, MINCED OVEN 375 DEGREE

RINSE CHICKEN; PAT DRY. CUT EACH WING AT JOINT TO MAKE 2 SECTIONS. PLACE THE WING PIECES IN A SINGLE LAYER IN A 13/9/2 INCH BAKING PAN. BAKE IN A 375 DEGREE OVEN FOR 20 MINUTES. DRAIN FAT FROM BAKING PAN.

FOR SAUCE, COMBINE REMAINING INGREDIENTS. BRUSH WINGS WITH SAUCE. BAKE 10 MINUTES. TURN WINGS OVER; BRUSH AGAIN WITH SAUCE. BAKE FOR 5 TO 10 MINUTES OR TILL CHICKEN IS TENDER. MAKE 16

CRUNCHY PARTY MIX

1 CUP MARGARINE OR BUTTER

3 TABLESPOONS WORCESTERSHIRE SAUCE

1/2 TEASPOON GARLIC POWDER

SEVERAL DROPS BOTTLED HOT PEPPER SAUCE

5 CUPS SMALL PRETZELS OR PRETZEL STICKS

4 CUPS ROUND TOASTED OAT CEREAL

4 CUPS BITE-SIZE WHEAT OR BRAN SQUARE CEREAL

4 CUPS BITE-SIZE RICE OR CORN SQUARE CEREAL OR BITE-SIZE SHREDDED

WHEAT BISCUITS

3 CUPS MIXED NUTS

IN A SAUCEPAN MIX MARGARINE, WORCESTERSHIRE SAUCE, GARLIC POWDER, AND PEPPER SAUCE. HEAT AND STIR TILL MARGARINE MELTS. IN A LARGE ROASTING PAN MIX PRETZELS, CEREALS, AND NUTS. DRIZZLE MARGARINE MIXTURE OVER CEREAL MIXTURE, TOSS TO COAT.

BAKE IN A 300 DEGREE OVEN FOR 45 MINUTES; STIRRING EVERY 15 MINUTES. SPREAD ON FOIL TO COOL. STORE IN AIRTIGHT CONTAINER. 40 SERVINGS

NACHOS

1/2 POUND BULK PORK SAUSAGE OR GROUND BEEF

1/2 CUP CHOPPED ONION

2 CLOVES GARLIC, MINCED

1 16-OUNCE CAN REFRIED BEANS

6 CUPS TORTILLA CHIPS

1/2 CUP SLICED PITTED OLIVES

1 4-OUNCE CAN DICED GREEN CHILI PEPPERS, DRAINED

1/2 CUPS SHREDDED CHEDDAR CHEESE OVEN 350 DEGREES

COOK MEAT, ONIONS, AND GARLIC TILL MEAT IS BROWN. DRAIN. STIR IN BEANS. ARRANGE HALF OF THE CHIPS ON EACH OF TWO 12-INCH OVENPROOF PLATTERS. LAYER HALF OF THE MEAT-BEAN MIXTURE, OLIVES, CHILI PEPPERS, AND CHEESE ON EACH PLATTER. BAKE IN 350 DEGREE OVEN FOR 5 TO 7 MINUTES OR TILL CHEESE MELTS. SERVE WITH AVOCADO DIP, DAIRY SOUR CREAM, AND SALSA, IF DESIRED. MAKE 8 SERVINGS.

POTATO SKINS

12 MEDIUM BAKING POTATOES

1/2 CUP MARGARINE OR BUTTER, MELTED

2 CUPS SHREDDED CHEDDAR OR MONTEREY JACK CHEESE (8 OUNCES)

GARLIC OR SEASONED SALT (OPTIONAL)

SALSA

SLICED GREEN ONION

PRICK POTATOES WITH A FORK. BAKE IN A 425 DEGREE OVEN FOR 40 TO 50 MINUTES TILL TENDER. CUT INTO QUARTERS. SCOOP OUT THE INSIDES (RESERVE FOR ANOTHER USE), LEAVING 1/2-INCH THICK SHELLS.

BRUSH BOTH SIDES OF POTATO SKINS WITH MARGARINE. PLACE, CUT SIDE UP, ON A LARGE BAKING SHEET. BAKE IN A 425 DEGREE OVEN FOR 10 TO 15 MINUTES OR TILL CRISP. SPRINKLE WITH CHEESE AND, IF DESIRED, SALT. BAKE ABOUT 2 MINUTES MORE OR TILL CHEESE MELTS. SERVE WITH SALSA AND GREEN ONION. MAKE 48

CREAMY DILL OR SEAFOOD DIP

1 8-OUNCE PACKAGE CREAM CHEESE, SOFTENED

1 8-OUNCE CARTON DAIRY SOUR CREAM

2 TABLESPOONS FINELY CHOPPED GREEN ONION

2 TEASPOON DRIED DILL WEED

1/2 TEASPOON SEASONED SALT OR SALT

VEGETABLE DIPPERS, ASSORTED CRACKERS, OR CHIPS

IN A MIXING BOWL BEAT CREAM CHEESE, SOUR CREAM, ONION, DILLWEED, AND SEASONED SALT WITH AN ELECTRIC MIXER TILL FLUFFY. CHILL UP TO 24 HOURS. IF DIP THICKENS AFTER CHILLING, STIR IN 1 OR 2 TABLESPOONS MILK. SERVE WITH VEGETABLE DIPPERS, CRACKERS, OR CHIPS. MAKE 2 CUPS (16 SERVINGS)

CREAMY SEAFOOD DIP: PREPARE AS ABOVE, EXCEPT STIR ONE 6 1/2 OUNCE CAN CLAMS, DRAINED, SHRIMP, DRAINED, OR CRABMEAT, DRAINED, FLAKED, AND CARTILAGE REMOVED, INTO BEATEN CHEESE MIXTURE.

HOT CHEESE DIP

1/4 CUP FINELY CHOPPED GREEN ONION

1 CLOVE GARLIC, MINCED

1/2 TEASPOON DRIED TARRAGON, CRUSHED

1 TABLESPOON MARGARINE OR BUTTER

1 TEASPOON CORNSTARCH

3/4 CUP BEER OR MILK

2 CUPS SHREDDED AMERICAN CHEESE

1 3-OUNCE PACKAGE CREAM CHEESE, CUT UP

FRENCH BREAD CUBES OR TORTILLA CHIPS

IN A SAUCEPAN COOK ONION, GARLIC, AND TARRAGON IN MARGARINE. STIR IN CORNSTARCH. ADD BEER ALL AT ONCE. COOK AND STIR TILL THICKENED AND BUBBLY. GRADUALLY ADD CHEESES, STIRRING TILL MELTED. SERVE WITH BREAD OR CHIPS. MAKE 2 CUPS (16 SERVINGS)

SHRIMP COCKTAIL

1 POUND FRESH OR FROZEN PEELED SHRIMP, COOKED,
DEVEINED, AND CHILLED

LETTUCE

COCKTAIL SAUCE (SEE RECIPE BELOW)

LEMON WEDGES

ARRANGE SHRIMP IN SIX LETTUCE-LINED COCKTAIL
CUPS OR GLASSES. SPOON 1 TABLESPOON OF THE
COCKTAIL SAUCE OVER EACH. SERVE WITH LEMON.
SERVE 6

COCKTAIL SAUCE

IN A BOWL COMBINE 3/4 CUP CHILI SAUCE; 2
TABLESPOON LEMON JUICE; 1 TABLESPOON
PREPARED HORSERADISH; 2 TEASPOON
WORCESTERSHIRE SAUCE; 1 GREEN ONION, SLICED,
OR 1/4 TEASPOON DRIED MINCED ONION; AND
SEVERAL DASHES HOT PEPPER SAUCE. COVER AND
STORE IN THE REFRIGERATOR UP TO 2 WEEKS.
SERVE WITH SHRIMP COCKTAIL. MAKE ABOUT 1
CUP (SIXTEEN 1-TABLESPOON SERVINGS).

BEVERAGES

APPLE CRANBERRY FRUIT PUNCH

64 OZ. BOTTLE APPLE CRANBERRY JUICE COCKTAIL

(CHILLED)

2 LITER BOTTLE GINGER ALE (CHILLED)

2 CUPS PINEAPPLE JUICE (CHILLED)

1 CUP SUGAR

1 TBS. ALMOND EXTRACT

MIX ALL INGREDIENTS TOGETHER; SERVE
IMMEDIATELY

ICE-CREAM PUNCH

2 QUARTS VANILLA ICE CREAM

1 1/2 CUPS COLD WATER

1 12-OUNCE CAN FROZEN LEMONADE CONCENTRATE
(THAWED)

2 1-LITER BOTTLES LEMONADE CARBONATED
BEVERAGE (CHILLED)

SPOON ICE CREAM BY TABLESPOON INTO A LARGE
PUNCH BOWL. ADD WATER AND LEMONADE
CONCENTRATE; STIR JUST TILL COMBINED. SLOWLY
POUR CARBONATED BEVERAGE DOWN THE SIDE OF
THE BOWL. STIR GENTLY TO MIX. MAKE 32 (ABOUT
4-OUNCE) SERVINGS.

SHERBET PUNCH; PREPARE AS ABOVE, EXCEPT
SUBSTITUTE LIME, ORANGE, LEMON, SHERBET FOR
ICE CREAM.

RED COAT RALLY

1 QT. 14 OZ. PINEAPPLE JUICE, CHILLED

3/4 CUP SUGAR

6 OZ. CAN FROZEN PINK LEMONADE CONCENTRATE,

DEFROSTED

2 1/4 CUPS WATER

1 QT. STRAWBERRY ICE CREAM

2 1/2 QT. GINGER ALE

IN PUNCH BOWL COMBINE PINEAPPLE JUICE,
SUGAR, LEMONADE AND WATER. ADD ICE CREAM.
STIR UNTIL BLENDED. STIR IN GINGER ALE. SERVE
AT ONCE.

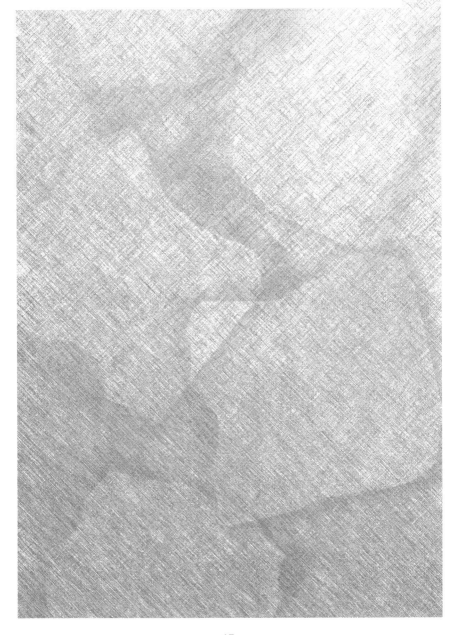

BREADS

BANANA-NUT BREAD

1 CUP MASHED RIPE BANANAS

1/3 CUP LOW-FAT BUTTERMILK

1/2 CUP PACKED BROWN SUGAR

1/4 CUP MARGARINE

1 EGG

2 CUPS SIFTED-ALL-PURPOSE FLOUR

1 TSP. BAKING POWER

1/2 TSP. BAKING SODA

1/2 CUP CHOPPED PECANS

PREHEAT OVEN TO 350 DEGREE F. LIGHTLY OIL 2 7X5 LOAF PANS. STIR TOGETHER MASHED BANANAS & BUTTERMILK; SET ASIDE. CREAM BROWN SUGAR & MARGARINE TOGETHER UNTIL LIGHT. BEAT IN EGG. ADD BANANA MIXTURE; BEAT WELL. SIFT TOGETHER FLOUR, BAKING POWDER, BAKING SODA, AND SALT; ADD ALL AT ONCE TO LIQUID INGREDIENTS. STIR UNTIL WELL BLENDED. STIR IN NUTS AND TURN INTO PREPARED PAN. BAKE 50-55 MINUTES OR UNTIL TOOTHPICK INSERTED COMES OUT CLEAN. COOL 5 MINUTES IN PAN. REMOVE FROM PAN AND COMPLETE COOLING ON A WIRE RACK BEFORE SLICING.

BISCUITS

2 CUPS ALL-PURPOSE FLOUR

1 TABLESPOON BAKING POWDER

2 TEASPOONS SUGAR

1/2 TEASPOON CREAM OF TARTAR

1/4 TEASPOON SALT

1/2 CUP SHORTENING, MARGARINE, OR BUTTER

2/3 CUP MILK OVEN 450 DEGREE

IN A BOWL STIR TOGETHER FLOUR, BAKING POWDER, SUGAR. CREAM OR TARTAR, AND SALT. CUT IN SHORTENING, MARGARINE, OR BUTTER TILL MIXTURE RESEMBLES COARSE CRUMBS. MAKE A WELL IN THE CENTER; ADD MILK ALL AT ONCE. STIR JUST TILL DOUGH CLINGS TOGETHER.

ON A LIGHTLY FLOURED SURFACE, KNEAD DOUGH GENTLY FOR 10 TO 12 STROKES. ROLL OR PAT DOUGH TO 1/2-INCH THICKNESS. CUT WITH A 2 1/2-INCH BISCUIT CUTTER, DIPPING CUTTER INTO FLOUR BETWEEN CUTS.

TRANSFER BISCUITS TO A BAKING SHEET. BAKE IN A 450 DEGREE OVEN FOR 10 TO 12 MINUTES OR TILL GOLDEN. SERVE WARM. MAKE 10.

BUTTERMILK BISCUITS:

PREPARE AS ABOVE, EXCEPT STIR 1/4 TEASPOON BAKING SODA INTO FLOUR MIXTURE AND SUBSTITUTE 3/4 CUP BUTTERMILK FOR THE MILK.

BUTTERMILK CORN BREAD

1 CUP CORN MEAL

1 CUP BUTTERMILK

2 TSP. BAKING POWDER

1/2 TSP. BAKING SODA

2 TBS. SUGAR

2 EGGS

1 TSP. SALT

4 TBS. COOKING OIL

1/2 CUP FLOUR

MIX ALL DRY INGREDIENTS ADD EGGS. BUTTERMILK, AND OIL. GREASE PAN. PRE-HEAT OVEN AT 425 DEGREE, BAKE 20 MINUTES OR UNTIL TOP IS GOLDEN BROWN.

CORN FRITTERS

1 8 3/4 -OUNCE CAN WHOLE KERNEL CORN

MILK

1 1/2 CUPS ALL-PURPOSE FLOUR

1/4 CUP CORNMEAL

2 TEASPOONS BAKING POWDER

1 BEATEN EGG

SHORTENING OR COOKING OIL FOR DEEP-FAT FRYING

DRAIN CORN, RESERVING LIQUID. ADD ENOUGH MILK TO RESERVED CORN LIQUID TO MAKE 1 CUP. IN A MIXING BOWL STIR TOGETHER FLOUR, CORNMEAL, BAKING POWDER, AND 1/2 TEASPOON SALT. ADD CORN, MILK MIXTURE, AND BEATEN EGG. STIR JUST TILL MOISTENED. DROP BATTER BY TABLESPOONS, FOUR OR FIVE AT A TIME, INTO DEEP HOT FAT (375 DEGREE).

COOK FOR 3 TO 4 MINUTES OR TILL GOLDEN BROWN, TURNING ONCE. DRAIN ON PAPER TOWELS. REPEAT. SERVE WARM. MAKE 24

APPLE FRITTERS:

PREPARE AS WITH CORN FRITTERS ON PREVIOUS
PAGE, EXCEPT SUBSTITUTE 1 CUP CHOPPED APPLE
FOR THE CORN AND USE 1 CUP MILK. STIR 2
TABLESPOONS SUGAR INTO FLOUR MIXTURE.
ROLL HOT FRITTERS IN A MIXTURE OF SUGAR AND
GROUND CINNAMON AFTER COOKING.

DINNER ROLLS

4 1/4 TO 4 3/4 ALL-PURPOSE FLOUR

1 PACKAGE ACTIVE DRY YEAST

1 CUP MILK

1/3 CUP SUGAR

1/3 CUP SHORTENING, MARGARINE, OR BUTTER

1/2 TEASPOON SALT

2 EGGS

COMBINE 2 CUPS OF THE FLOUR AND THE YEAST. HEAT AND STIR MILK, SUGAR, SHORTENING, AND SALT JUST TILL WARM (120 DEGREE TO 130 DEGREE) AND SHORTENING ALMOST MELTS. ADD TO FLOUR MIXTURE ALONG WITH EGGS. BEAT WITH AN ELECTRIC MIXTURE ON LOW SPEED FOR 30 SECONDS, SCRAPING BOWL CONSTANTLY. BEAT ON HIGH SPEED FOR 3 MINUTES. USING A SPOON, STIR IN AS MUCH OF THE REMAINING FLOUR AS YOU CAN. TURN DOUGH OUT ONTO A LIGHTLY FLOURED SURFACE. KNEAD IN ENOUGH REMAINING FLOUR TO MAKE A MODERATELY STIFF DOUGH THAT IS SMOOTH AND ELASTIC (6 TO 8 MINUTES TOTAL). SHAPE DOUGH INTO A BALL. PLACE DOUGH IN A GREASED BOWL; TURN ONCE TO GREASE SURFACE. COVER AND LET RISE IN A WARM PLACE TILL DOUBLE (ABOUT 1 HOUR).

PUNCH DOUGH DOWN. TURN OUT ONTO A LIGHTLY FLOURED SURFACE. DIVIDE DOUGH IN HALF. COVER AND LET REST FOR 10 MINUTES. SHAPE THE DOUGH INTO DESIRED ROLLS. COVER AND LET RISE IN A WARM PLACE TILL NEARLY DOUBLE (ABOUT 30 MINUTES).

BAKE IN A 375 DEGREE OVEN FOR 12 TO 15 MINUTES OR TILL GOLDEN BROWN. MAKE 24 TO 32 ROLLS.

EASY-DO SWEET ROLLS

PREPARATION TIME-10 MINUTES

RISING TIME-1 1/2 TO 2 HOURS

BAKING TIME-20 TO 30 MINUTES

1 1/2 PKG DRY YEAST

1 CUP WARM WATER

1/3 CUP NONFAT DRY MILK

1/2 CUP SUGAR

1/4 CUP COOKING OIL

2 TSP SALT

1 EGG

3 1/2 TO 4 CUPS FLOUR

MEASURE WATER INTO LARGE BOWL. SPRINKLE YEAST OVER WATER. ADD DRY MILK, SUGAR, OIL, EGG, SALT AND ABOUT 1 1/2 CUPS FLOUR. BLEND WELL. BEAT 3 MINUTES AT MEDIUM SPEED OF MIXER. BY HAND GRADUALLY ADD REMAINING FLOUR TO FORM A STIFF DOUGH, BEATING WELL AFTER EACH ADDITION. COVER; LET REST 15 MINUTES. TOSS DOUGH ON FLOURED SURFACE UNTIL NO LONGER STICKY.

KNEAD 1 MINUTE. SHAPE. LET RISE UNTIL DOUBLE IN SIZE. BAKE IN A 375 DEGREE OVEN FOR 20 TO 30 MINUTES OR TILL GOLDEN BROWN. MAKE 24 ROLLS.

FRENCH TOAST

2 BEATEN EGGS

1/2 CUP MILK

1/4 TEASPOON VANILLA

1/8 TEASPOON GROUND CINNAMON

5 1-INCH-THICK SLICES FRENCH BREAD OR 6 SLICES DRY WHITE BREAD

MARGARINE, BUTTER, OR COOKING OIL

MAPLE-FLAVORED SYRUP (OPTIONAL)

IN A SHALLOW BOWL BEAT TOGETHER EGGS, MILK, VANILLA, AND CINNAMON. DIP BREAD INTO EGG MIXTURE, COATING BOTH SIDES (IF USING FRENCH BREAD, LET SOAK IN EGG MIXTURE ABOUT 30 SECONDS ON EACH SIDE) IN A SKILLET OR ON A GRIDDLE COOK BREAD ON BOTH SIDES IN A SMALL AMOUNT OF HOT MARGARINE, BUTTER, OR OIL OVER MEDIUM HEAT FOR 2 TO 3 MINUTES ON EACH SIDE OR TILL GOLDEN BROWN. ADD MORE MARGARINE AS NEEDED. SERVE WITH MAPLE-FLAVORED SYRUP, IF DESIRED. MAKE 5 OR 6 SLICES.

HUSH PUPPIES

1 BEATEN EGG

1/2 CUP BUTTERMILK OR SOUR MILK

1/4 CUP SLICED GREEN ONION

1 CUP CORNMEAL

1/4 CUP ALL-PURPOSE FLOUR

2 TEASPOONS SUGAR

3/4 TEASPOON BAKING POWDER

1/4 TEASPOON BAKING SODA

SHORTENING OR COOKING OIL FOR DEEP-FAT FRYING

IN A BOWL STIR TOGETHER EGG, BUTTERMILK OR SOUR MILK, AND ONION. IN ANOTHER BOWL COMBINE CORNMEAL, FLOUR, SUGAR, BAKING POWDER, BAKING SODA AND 1/4 TEASPOON SALT. ADD EGG MIXTURE TO CORNMEAL MIXTURE; STIR JUST TILL MOISTENED. DROP BATTER BY TABLESPOON OR FLAT LIKE A PANCAKE INTO DEEP HOT FAT (375 DEGREE). FRY ABOUT 3 MINUTES OR TILL GOLDEN, TURNING ONCE. DRAIN ON PAPER TOWELS. MAKE 14 TO 18.

PANCAKES

1 CUP ALL-PURPOSE FLOUR

1 TABLESPOON SUGAR

2 TEASPOONS BAKING POWDER

1/4 TEASPOON SALT

1 BEATEN EGG

1 CUP MILK

2 TABLESPOONS COOKING OIL

IN A MIXING BOWL STIR TOGETHER FLOUR, SUGAR, BAKING POWDER, AND SALT. IN ANOTHER MIXING BOWL COMBINE EGG, MILK, AND COOKING OIL. ADD TO FLOUR MIXTURE ALL AT ONCE. STIR MIXTURE JUST TILL BLENDED BUT STILL SLIGHTLY LUMPY.

POUR ABOUT 1/4 CUP BATTER ONTO A HOT, LIGHTLY GREASED GRIDDLE OR HEAVY SKILLET FOR EACH STANDARD-SIZE PANCAKE OR ABOUT 1 TABLESPOON BATTER FOR EACH DOLLAR-SIZE PANCAKE. COOK TILL PANCAKE ARE GOLDEN BROWN, TURNING TO COOK SECOND SIDES WHEN PANCAKES HAVE BUBBLE SURFACES AND SLIGHTLY DRY EDGES. MAKE 8 TO 10 STANDARD SIZE OR 36 DOLLAR-SIZE PANCAKES.

WAFFLES

1 3/4 CUPS ALL-PURPOSE FLOUR

1 TABLESPOON BAKING POWDER

1/4 TEASPOON SALT

2 EGG YOLKS

1 3/4 CUPS MILK

1/2 CUP COOKING OIL

2 EGG WHITES

IN A MIXING BOWL COMBINE FLOUR, BAKING POWDER, AND SALT. IN ANOTHER BOWL BEAT EGG YOLKS SLIGHTLY. BEAT IN MILK AND OIL. ADD EGG YOLK MIXTURE TO FLOUR MIXTURE ALL AT ONCE. STIR JUST TILL COMBINED BUT STILL SLIGHTLY LUMPY.

IN A SMALL BOWL BEAT EGG WHITES TILL STIFF PEAKS FORM (TIP STAND STRAIGHT). GENTLY FOLD BEATEN EGG WHITES INTO FLOUR AND EGG YOLK MIXTURE, LEAVING A FEW FLUFFS OF EGG WHITE. DO NOT OVERMIX. POUR 1 TO 1 1/4 CUPS BATTER ONTO GRIDS OF A PRE-HEATED, LIGHTLY GREASED WAFFLE BAKER. CLOSE LID QUICKLY; DO NOT OPEN DURING BAKING. BAKE ACCORDING TO MANUFACTURER'S DIRECTIONS. WHEN DONE, USE A FORK TO LIFT WAFFLE OFF GRID. REPEAT WITH REMAINING BATTER. MAKE 3 OR 4 WAFFLES

CAKES

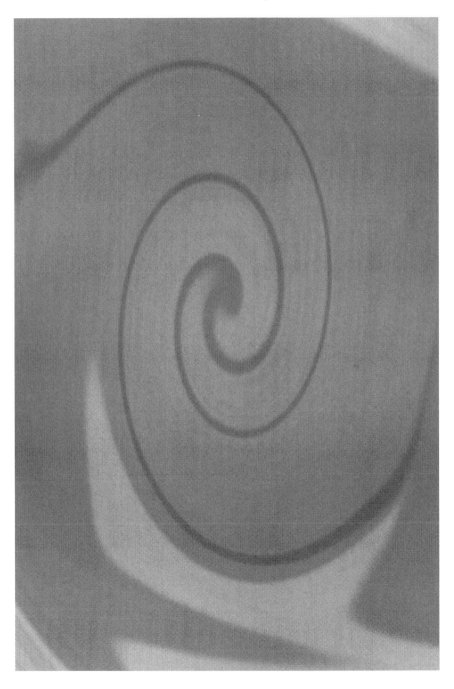

BROWN SUGAR POUND CAKE

1/2 CUP BUTTER OR MARGARINE

1 CUP SHORTENING

1 CUP SUGAR

1 1-POUND BOX LIGHT BROWN SUGAR

1 1/2 TEASPOONS VANILLA

5 EGGS

3 1/2 CUPS SIFTED FLOUR

1 TEASPOON SALT

1 CUP EVAPORATED MILK

1 CUP FLAKED COCONUT

1 CUP CHOPPED NUTS

CREAM BUTTER AND SHORTENING; GRADUALLY ADD SUGAR AND BROWN SUGAR, BEATING UNTIL LIGHT AND FLUFFY. BLEND IN VANILLA. ADD EGGS, ONE AT A TIME, BEATING WELL AFTER EACH ADDITION. SIFT TOGETHER FLOUR, BAKING POWDER AND SALT; ADD TO CREAMED MIXTURE ALTERNATELY WITH EVAPORATED MILK, MIXING WELL. FOLD IN COCONUT AND NUTS. POUR INTO A WELL-GREASED AND FLOURED 10-INCH TUBE PAN. BAKE AT 325 DEGREE OVEN 1 HOUR AND 40 MINUTES, OR UNTIL DONE.

GLAZE:

1/3 CUP BUTTER OR MARGARINE

1 CUP FIRMLY PACKED LIGHT BROWN SUGAR

1/4 CUP EVAPORATED MILK

1 TEASPOON VANILLA

1/2 CUP CHOPPED NUTS

MELT BUTTER OVER MEDIUM HEAT IN SAUCEPAN;
BLEND IN SUGAR. ADD MILK AND BRING TO
A ROLLING BOIL; BOIL 2 MINUTES. TURN OFF
HEAT; COOL. ADD VANILLA AND BEAT UNTIL OF
SPREADING CONSISTENCY WITH GLAZE. ADD
CHOPPED NUTS OVER GLAZE.

CARAMEL CAKE

1 CUP SOUR CREAM

1/4 CUP MILK

2/3 CUP BUTTER OR MARGARINE

1 3/4 CUPS SUGAR

2 EGGS

1 TEASPOON VANILLA

1 TEASPOON ALMOND EXTRACT

2 1/4 CUPS ALL-PURPOSE FLOUR

2 1/2 TEASPOONS BAKING POWDER

1 TEASPOON SALT, OPTIONAL

COMBINE SOUR CREAM AND MILK, SET ASIDE.
HEAT OVEN TO 350 DEGREE. GREASE AND FLOUR
2 ROUND 9X1 1/2-INCHES. MIX, BUTTER, SUGAR,
EGGS, VANILLA AND ALMOND EXTRACT IN LARGE
MIXING BOWL UNTIL FLUFFY. BEAT ON HIGH SPEED,
SCRAPING BOWL OCCASIONALLY, 5 MINUTES.
COMBINE FLOUR, BAKING POWDER AND SALT, ADD
TO CREAMED MIXTURE ALTERNATELY WITH SOUR
CREAM, BEGINNING AND ENDING WITH FLOUR
MIXTURE. POUR BATTER INTO PREPARED PAN.

BAKE UNTIL WOODEN TOOTH PICK INSERTED IN

CENTER COMES OUT CLEAN, 30 TO 35 MINUTES.
COOL LAYERS 10 MINUTES, REMOVE FROM PAN
AND COOL COMPLETELY. FILL AND FROST LAYERS
WITH CARMEL FROSTING WHICH IS SHOWN ON THE
NEXT PAGE.

CARAMEL FROSTING

3 CUPS SUGAR, DIVIDED

1 TABLESPOON ALL-PURPOSE FLOUR

1 CUP MILK

3/4 CUP BUTTER OR MARGARINE

1 TEASPOON VANILLA

SPRINKLE 1/2 CUP SUGAR IN A SHALLOW, HEAVY 3 1/2 QUART DUTCH OVEN; PLACE OVER MEDIUM HEAT. COOK, STIRRING CONSTANTLY, UNTIL SUGAR DISSOLVES AND SYRUP IS LIGHT GOLDEN BROWN. REMOVE FROM HEAT. COMBINE REMAINING 2 1/2 CUPS SUGAR AND FLOUR, STIRRING WELL; ADD MILK AND BRING TO A BOIL, STIRRING CONSTANTLY. GRADUALLY POUR ONE-FOURTH HOT MIXTURE INTO CARAMELIZED SUGAR, STIRRING CONSTANTLY; ADD REMAINING HOT MIXTURE (MIXTURE WILL LUMP), BUT CONTINUE STIRRING UNTIL SMOOTH. RETURN TO HEAT. COVER MIXTURE. COOK OVER LOW HEAT 2 MINUTES. UNCOVER AND COOK (WITHOUT STIRRING) OVER MEDIUM HEAT UNTIL CANDY THERMOMETER REACHES 238 DEGREE. ADD BUTTER, STIRRING TO BLEND. REMOVE FROM HEAT AND COOL WITHOUT STIRRING UNTIL TEMPERATURE DROPS TO 110

DEGREE (ABOUT 1 HOUR). ADD VANILLA AND BEAT WITH WOODEN SPOON OR WITH AN ELECTRIC HAND MIXTURE UNTIL IT IS OF SPREADING CONSISTENCY.

CHOCOLATE CAKE

1 2/3 CUPS GOLD METAL FLOUR

1 1/2 CUPS SUGAR

2/3 CUP HERSHEY'S COCOA

1 1/2 TSP. SODA

1 TSP. SALT

1/2 CUP SHORTENING

1 1/2 CUPS BUTTERMILK

1 TSP. VANILLA

2 EGGS

HEAT OVEN TO 350 DEGREE. GREASE AND FLOUR 2 ROUND LAYER PANS, 8 OR 9X1 1/2, OR OBLONG PAN, 13X9X2". IN LARGE MIXING BOWL COMBINE ALL INGREDIENTS. BLEND ON LOW SPEED 30 SEC., SCRAPING SIDES AND BOTTOM OF BOWL. BEAT 3 MIN. ON MED. SPEED, SCRAPING BOWL FREQUENTLY. POUR INTO PREPARED PAN(S). BAKE LAYERS 30 TO 35 MIN., OBLONG 35 TO 40 MIN. OR UNTIL WOODEN PICK INSERTED IN CENTER OF CAKE COMES OUT CLEAN. FROST WITH FOLLOWING CHOCOLATE ICING.

CHOCOLATE ICING:

1 CUP BUTTER OR MARGARINE

1 1/2 TEASPOONS VANILLA

3 1/2 CUPS SIFTED POWDER SUGAR

3 1/2 CUPS HERSHEY COCOA

3 TO 4 TABLESPOONS MILK

BEAT BUTTER OR MARGARINE, VANILLA WITH
AN ELECTRIC MIXER ON MEDIUM SPEED FOR 30
SECONDS. SLOWLY ADD HALF OF THE POWDER
SUGAR AND COCOA, BEATING WELL. ADD
2 TABLESPOONS MILK. GRADUALLY BEAT IN
REMAINING POWDERED SUGAR AND COCOA
AND REMAINING MILK TO MAKE OF SPREADING
CONSISTENCY. FROSTS TOPS AND SIDES OF TWO
8- OR 9-INCH CAKE LAYERS.

GERMAN CHOCOLATE CAKE

1 4-OUNCE PACKAGE GERMAN SWEET COOKING

CHOCOLATE

1 2/3 CUPS ALL-PURPOSE FLOUR

1 1/3 CUPS SUGAR

1 TEASPOON BAKING POWDER

1/2 TEASPOON BAKING SODA

2/3 CUP BUTTERMILK OR SOUR MILK

1/2 CUP MARGARINE OR BUTTER, SOFTENED, OR
SHORTENING

1 TEASPOON VANILLA

3 EGGS

IN A SAUCEPAN COMBINE CHOCOLATE AND 1/3
CUP WATER; COOK AND STIR OVER LOW HEAT
TILL MELTED. COOL. IN A BOWL COMBINE FLOUR,
SUGAR, BAKING POWDER, BAKING SODA, AND
1/8 TEASPOON SALT. ADD CHOCOLATE MIXTURE,
MILK, MARGARINE, AND VANILLA. BEAT WITH AN
ELECTRIC MIXER ON LOW TO MEDIUM SPEED TILL
COMBINED. BEAT TILL COMBINED. BEAT ON HIGH
SPEED FOR 2 MINUTES.

ADD EGGS AND BEAT 2 MINUTES MORE. POUR
INTO 2 GREASED AND FLOURED 8X1 1/2 OR 9X1
1/2-INCH ROUND BAKING PANS. BAKE IN A 350

DEGREE OVEN FOR 30 TO 40 MINUTES OR TILL A TOOTHPICK COMES OUT CLEAN. COOL ON RACKS 10 MINUTES. REMOVE FROM PANS. COOL ON RACKS. FROST WITH THE FOLLOWING COCONUT-PECAN FROSTING. MAKE 12 SERVINGS.

COCONUT-PECAN FROSTING:

1 EGG

1 5-OUNCE CAN (2/3 CUP) EVAPORATED MILK

2/3 CUP SUGAR

1/4 CUP MARGARINE OR BUTTER

1 1/3 CUPS FLAKED COCONUT

1/2 CUP CHOPPED PECANS

IN A SAUCEPAN BEAT EGG SLIGHTLY. STIR IN MILK, SUGAR, AND MARGARINE. COOK AND STIR OVER MEDIUM HEAT ABOUT 12 MINUTES OR TILL TICKENED AND BUBBLY. SITR IN COCONUT AND PECANS. COOL THIROUGHLY. SPREAD ON CAKE. FROST TOP OF ONE 13X9-INCH CAKE OR TOPS OF TWO 8 OR 9-INCH CAKE LAYERS.

PINEAPPLE UPSIDE-DOWN CAKE

2 TABLESPOON MARGARINE OR BUTTER

1/3 CUP PACKED BROWN SUGAR

1 8-OUNCE CAN PINEAPPLE SLICES, DRAINED AND HALVED

4 MARASCHINO CHERRIES, HALVED

1 1/3 CUPS ALL-PURPOSE FLOUR

2/3 CUP SUGAR

2 TEASPOONS BAKING POWDER

2/3 CUP MILK

1/4 CUP MARGARINE OR BUTTER, SOFTENED

1 EGG

1 TEASPOON VANILLA

IN A BOWL COMBINE FLOUR, SUGAR, AND BAKING POWDER. ADD MILK, MARGARINE OR BUTTER, EGG, AND VANILLA. BEAT WITH AN ELECTRIC MIXER ON LOW SPEED TILL COMBINED. BEAT ON MEDIUM SPEED FOR 1 MINUTE. MELT MARGARINE IN A 9X1 1/2-INCH ROUND BAKING PAN. STIR IN SUGAR AND 1 TABLESPOON WATER. ARRANGE PINEAPPLE AND CHERRIES IN THE PAN. SPOON THE MIXED BATTER INTO THE PAN. BAKE IN A 350 DEGREE OVEN FOR 30 TO 35 MINUTES OR TILL A TOOTHPICK INSERTED NEAR THE CENTER COMES OUT CLEAN. COOL ON A WIRE RACK FOR 5 MINUTES. LOOSEN SIDES; INVERT ONTO A PLATE. SERVE WARM. SERVES 8.

LEMON CAKE

3/4 CUP COOKING OIL

3/4 CUP COLD WATER

4 EGGS

1 PKG. LEMON CAKE MIX

1 PKG. INSTANT LEMON PUDDING

MIX OIL, WATER, & EGGS. BEAT UNTIL FROTHY, AT LEAST 4 MINUES. BLEND IN 1 PKG. LEMON CAKE MIX & INSTANT LEMON PUDDING & BLEND. BAKE 50 MINUTES (TILL TOOTHPICK COMES OUT WITH NO DOUGH) IN 350 DEGREES OVEN.

PREPARE JUICE FROM 2 LEMONS (1/2 CUP) AND 1 1/2 CUPS CONFECTIONARY SUGAR AND BEAT WITH MIXER UNTIL WELL BLENDED.

PUNCH HOLES IN CAKE WHILE HOT AND STILL IN CAKE PAN. SLOWLY POUR THE LEMON JUICE MIXTURE THROUGH CAKE. COOL CAKE. REMOVE FROM PAN.

POUND CAKE

1 CUP BUTTER

 2 3/4 CUP SUGAR

1/2 CUP CRISCO

1 TSP. LEMON FLAVORING

1 TSP. VANILLA FLAVORING

5 LARGE EGGS

1 CUP MILK

3 CUPS VELVET CAKE FLOUR

CREAM TOGETHER FIRST 5 INGREDIENTS UNTIL
FLUFFY. ADD EGGS, ONE AT A TIME, UNTIL WELL
MIXED. ADD 1 CUP MILK AND FLOUR; MIX WELL.
DO NOT PREHEAT OVEN. BAKE IN TUBE PAN FOR
1 HOUR AND 20 MINUTES AT 350 DEGREE. FROST
WITH THE FOLLOWING BUTTER FROSTING, IF
DESIRED.

BUTTER FROSTING:

1/3 CUP BUTTER OR MARGARINE

4 1/2 CUPS SIFTED POWDERED SUGAR

1/4 CUP MILK

1 1/2 TEASPOONS VANILLA

MILK (IF NEEDED)

IN A BOWL BEAT BUTTER OR MARGARINE TILL FLUFFY. GRADUALLY ADD 2 CUPS OF THE POWDERED SUGAR, BEATING WELL. SLOWLY BEAT IN THE 1/4 CUP MILK AND VANILLA.

SLOWLY BEAT IN REMAINING SUGAR. BEAT IN ADDITIONAL MILK, IF NEEDED, TO MAKE SPREADING CONSISTENCY. TINT WITH FOOD COLORING, IF DESIRED. FROSTS TOPS AND SIDES.

SOCK-IT-TO-ME CAKE

1 PACKAGE DUNCAN HINES BUTTER RECIPE GOLDEN CAKE MIX

1 CUP (8 OUNCES) DAIRY SOUR CREAM

1/3 CUP CRISCO OIL OR PURITAN OIL

1/4 CUP SUGAR

1/4 CUP WATER

4 EGGS

FILLING:2 TABLESPOONS RESERVED CAKE MIX

2 TEASPOONS CINNAMON

2 TABLESPOONS BROWN SUGAR

1 CUP FINELY CHOPPED PECANS

PREHEAT OVEN TO 375 DEGREE:

COMBINE FILLING INGREDIENTS AND SET ASIDE. IN A LARGE BOWL BLEND CAKE MIX, SOUR CREAM, OIL, 1/4 CUP SUGAR, WATER AND EGGS. BEAT AT HIGH SPEED FOR 2 MINUTES. POUR 2/3 OF THE BATTER IN A GREASED AND FLOURED 10-INCH TUBE OR BUNDT PAN.

SPRINKLE FILLING INGREDIENTS OVER BATTER IN PAN. SPREAD REMAINING BATTER EVENLY OVER FILLING MIXTURE.

BAKE AT 375 DEGREE FOR 45-55 MINUTES, UNTIL CAKE SPRINGS BACK WHEN TOUCHED LIGHTLY.

COOL RIGHT SIDE UP FOR ABOUT 25 MINUTES,
THEN REMOVE FROM PAN.

GLAZE:

BLEND 1 CUP CONFECTIONER'S SUGAR AND 2
TABLESPOON MILK. DRIZZLE OVER CAKE.

DESSERT

AMBROSIA

1 CAN (20 OZ.) DOLE CHUNK PINEAPPLE IN JUICE OR SYRUP

1 CAN (11 OZ.) DOLE MANDARIN ORANGE SEGMENTS

1-1/2 CUPS SEEDLESS GRAPES

1 CUP MINIATURE MARSHMALLOWS

1 CUP FLAKED COCONUT

1/2 CUP NUTS

3/4 CUP DAIRY SOUR CREAM

1 TABLESPOON SUGAR

DRAIN PINEAPPLE. DRAIN ORANGES. COMBINE
PINEAPPLE; ORANGES, GRAPES, MARSHMALLOWS,
COCONUT, AND NUTS. MIX SOUR CREAM AND
SUGAR. STIR INTO FRUIT MIXTURE. CHILL. MAKE 4
TO 6 SERVINGS.

BANANA PUDDING

1 PKG (4 SERVING SIZE) JELLO VANILLA OR BANANA CREAM FLAVOR COOK AND SERVE PUDDING AND PIE FILLING

2 EGG YOLKS

2 1/2 CUPS MILK

30-35 VANILLA WAFERS

2 LARGE BANANAS, SLICED

2 EGG WHITES

DASH OF SALT

1/4 CUP SUGAR

HEAT OVEN TO 425 DEGREE F.

COMBINE PUDDING MIX, EGGS YOLKS AND MILK IN MEDIUM SAUCE PAN. COOK ON MEDIUM HEAT UNTIL MIXTURE COMES TO FULL BOIL. STIRRING CONSTANTLY. REMOVE FROM HEAT. ARRANGE LAYER OF VANILLA WAFERS ON BOTTOM AND UP SIDES OF A 1-1/2 QUART BAKING DISH. ADD 1 LAYER OF BANANA SLICES; TOP WITH 1/3 OF THE PUDDING. CONTINUE LAYERING WAFERS, BANANA AND PUDDING, ENDING WITH PUDDING.

BEAT EGG WHITES AND SALT WITH ELECTRIC MIXER UNTIL FOAMY. GRADUALLY ADD SUGAR, BEATING UNTIL STIFF PEAKS FOAM. SPOON LIGHTLY ON

PUDDING, SEALING EDGES WELL.

BAKE 5 TO 10 MINUTES OR UNTIL MERINGUE IS LIGHTLY BROWNED. SERVE WARM OR REFRIGERATE UNTIL READY TO SERVE. 8 SERVINGS.

CANDIED SWEET POTATOES (BAKED)

6 MEDIUM SWEET POTATOES

2 CUPS DOMINO LIGHT BROWN SUGAR

1 TEASPOON SALT

1/2 CUP BUTTER OR MARGARINE

1/2 CUP WATER

PARBOIL POTATOES 12 MINUTES. PEEL AND CUT LENGTHWISE. PLACE IN BUTTERED BAKING PAN. COMBINE SUGAR, SALT, BUTTER OR MARGARINE, AND WATER. BOIL 3 MINUTES. POUR SYRUP OVER POTATOES. BAKE IN MODERATE OVEN 350 DEGREE FOR 1 TO 1-1/4 HOUR. BASTE OCCASIONALLY. YIELD 6 SERVINGS.

CANDIED SWEET POTATOES (TOP STOVE)

3 OR 4 MEDIUM SWEET POTATOES

WATER

1 CUP SUGAR

1 STICK BUTTER OR MARGARINE

1/2 TEASPOON NUTMEG

1/3 TEASPOON CINNAMON

SLICE SWEET POTATOES IN SMALL PIECES. USING JUST ENOUGH WATER TO COVER, PLACE IN POT AND BOIL UNTIL TENDER. ADD SUGAR, BUTTER OR MARGARINE, NUTMEG AND CINNAMON. COOK UNTIL SYRUPY. SERVE 3 OR 4.

PISTACHIO FLUFF

1 BOX INSTANT PISTACHIO PUDDING & PIE FILLING

(FOLLOW DIRECTIONS ON THE BOX FOR PREPARATION)

FOLD IN:

1 8 OZ. TUB COOL WHIP

1 CAN CRUSHED PINEAPPLE (DRAINED)

SMALL MARSHMALLOWS

WALNUT PIECES

RICE PUDDING

2 CUPS COOKED RICE

2-2/3 CUPS MILK (1 CAN PET MILK & WATER)

1/2 CUP RAISINS

2 EGGS

1 CUP SUGAR

2 TABLESPOONS MELTED BUTTER

3/4 TEASPOON SALT

MIX TOGETHER RICE, MILK AND RAISINS IN
GREASED 1-1/2 QUART CASSEROLE. IN MIXING
BOWL STIR TOGETHER EGGS, SUGAR, BUTTER AND
SALT. POUR OVER RICE MIXTURE AND MIX WELL.
BAKE AT 350 DEGREE OVEN FOR 1 HOUR OR UNTIL
CRUST IS GOLDEN BROWN. PUDDING WILL SET AS IT
COOLS. MAKE 6 SERVINGS.

RUM BALLS

1 CUP PECANS

1 CUP VANILLA WAFERS CRUMBS

2 TABLESPOONS COCOA

1 CUP POWDERED SUGAR

1-1/2 TABLESPOONS WHITE KARO SYRUP

1/4 CUP RUM

MIX ALL INGREDIENTS TOGETHER. USING ABOUT
1 ROUNDED TEASPOON OF THE MIXTURE,
FORM SMALL BALLS. ROLL IN EXTRA POWDERED
SUGAR AND STORE IN TIGHTLY COVERED
CONTAINER, MAKING SURE THEY ARE NOT
CROWDED TOGETHER. STORE IN TIGHTLY COVERED
CONTAINER FOR FOUR WEEKS.

EGGS, CHEESE & LEGUMES

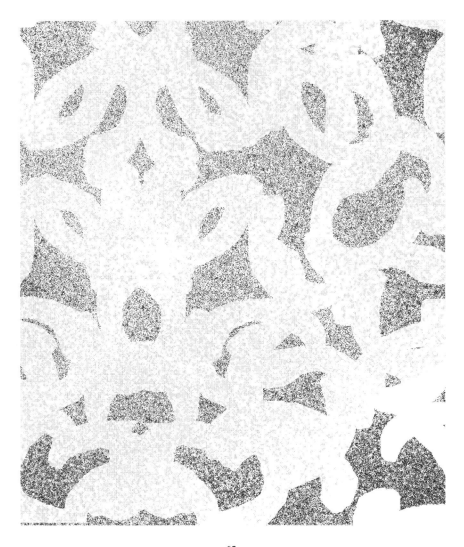

BLACKEYE PEAS

1 TURKEY WING OR HAM HOCK

1 LB. BLACKEYE PEAS

CRUSHED RED PEPPERS TO TASTE (OPTIONAL)

SMALL ONION (DICED)

CLOVE GARLIC OR GARLIC POWDER

1 TEAS. BLACK PEPPER

1 TABLESPOON SUGAR

SALT TO TASTE

LET BLACKEYE PEAS SOAK OVERNIGHT IN COLD WATER. COOK TURKEY WING OR HAM HOCK FOR ABOUT 30 MINUTES. THEN ADD BLACKEYE PEAS, SALT, RED AND/OR BLACK PEPPER, GARLIC, SUGAR AND COOK ABOUT 2 HOURS OR UNTIL THE CONSISTENCY IS LIKE THICK SOUP. SERVE 4.

DEVILED EGGS

6 HARD BOILED EGGS

1/4 CUP MAYONNAISE OR SALAD DRESSING

1 TEASPOON PREPARED MUSTARD

1 TEASPOON VINEGAR

PAPRIKA OR PARSLEY SPRIGS (OPTIONAL)

HALVE HARD-COOKED EGGS LENGTHWISE AND REMOVE YOLKS. PLACE YOLKS IN A BOWL; MASH WITH A FOLK. ADD MAYONNAISE, MUSTARD, AND VINEGAR; MIX WELL. SEASON WITH SALT AND PEPPER. STUFF EGG WHITE HALVES WITH YOLK MIXTURE. GARNISH WITH PAPRIKA OR PARSLEY, IF DESIRED. MAKE 12 SERVINGS.

MACARONI AND CHEESE

6 CUPS WATER

1 TABLESPOON SALT

2 CUPS MACARONI

1/4 CUP BUTTER PLUS 2 TABLESPOONS, SOFTENED

2 LARGE EGGS

2 CUPS EVAPORATED MILK

1/2 TO 1 TEASPOON SALT

2 DASHES TABASCO SAUCE

1 POUND EXTRA-SHARP CHEDDAR CHEESE, GRATED AND MIXED WITH ONE-HALF CUP GRATED AMERICAN CHEESE

ONE-HALF TEASPOON PAPRIKA

PREHEAT OVEN TO 350 DEGREES.

PUT THE WATER AND (1 TABLESPOON) SALT IN A HEAVY SAUCEPAN AND BRING TO A BOIL.

SLOWLY STIR IN THE MACRONI. BOIL FOR 12 MINUTES, STIRRING CONSTANTLY. THE MACARONI SHOULD BE FIRM BUT TENDER. POUR THE MACARONI INTO A COLANDER AND RINSE WITH A LITTLE COLD WATER. DRAIN. TOSS THE MACARONI WITH THE BUTTER AND SET ASIDE. IN A SMALL BOWL, BEAT THE EGGS UNTIL LIGHT YELLOW. ADD

THE MILK, SALT, AND TABASCO SAUCE. IN A LARGE BUTTERED CASSEROLE DISH, ALTERNATE LAYERS OF THE COOKED MACARONI WITH LAYERS OF THE MIXED CHEESES, ENDING WITH THE CHEESE ON TOP. POUR THE THE EGG MIXTURE SLOWLY AND EVENLY OVER THE MACARONI AND CHEESE. SPRINKLE WITH THE PAPRIKA. BAKE FOR 30 TO 40 MINUTES, UNTIL THE CUSTARD IS SET AND THE TOP IS BUBBLY AND GOLDEN BROWN. SERVE 8.

RED BEANS AND RICE

1 TURKEY WING OR HAM HOCK

1 LB. RED OR KIDNEY BEANS

CRUSHED RED PEPPERS TO TASTE (OPTIONAL)

SMALL ONION (DICED)

CLOVE GARLIC OR GARLIC POWDER

BLACK PEPPER

1 TABLESPOON SUGAR

SALT TO TASTE

LET RED OR KIDNEY BEANS SOAK OVERNIGHT IN COLD WATER. COOK TURKEY WING OR HAM HOCK FOR ABOUT 30 MINUTES. THEN ADD RED OR KIDNEY BEANS, SALT, RED AND/OR BLACK PEPPER, GARLIC, SUGAR AND COOK ABOUT 2 HOURS OR UNTIL THE CONSISTENCY IS LIKE THICK SOUP. SERVE OVER THE FOLLOWING RICE RECIPE.

RICE

1 CUP RICE

2 1/4 CUPS WATER

1 TSP SALT

2 TSP. BUTTER

COMBINE RICE, SALT, WATER AND BUTTER IN A
SAUCEPAN. BRING TO A BOIL, COVER AND REDUCE
HEAT. SIMMER 20 MINUTES. REMOVE FROM HEAT.
LET STAND COVERED 5 MINUTES OR UNTIL WATER
IS ABSORBED. FLUFF WITH FORK.

SERVE 4

WESTERN OMELET

4 EGGS

1/2 CUP MILK

1 TABLESPOON MARGARINE OR BUTTER

1/2 CUP ONIONS (DICED)

1/2 CUP GREEN PEPPERS (DICED)

1/2 CUP DICED CHEDDAR OR AMERICAN CHEESE

SALT TO TASTE

BLACK PEPPER

IN A BOWL COMBINE EGGS, MILK, SALT, AND BLACK PEPPER. USING A FOLK, BEAT TILL COMBINED BUT NOT FROTHY. STIR IN CHEESE. IN A 8- OR 10-INCH SKILLET WITH FLARED SIDES, HEAT MARGARINE OR BUTTER. LIFT AND TILT THE PAN TO COAT THE SIDES. ADD ONIONS AND GREEN PEPPERS AND COOK FOR 1 MINUTE.

ADD EGG MIXTURE TO SKILLET; COOK OVER MEDIUM HEAT. AS EGGS SET, RUN A SPATULA AROUND THE EDGE OF THE SKILLET, LIFTING EGGS AND LETTING UNCOOKED PORTION

FLOW UNDERNEATH. WHEN EGGS ARE SET BUT STILL SHINEY, REMOVE FROM THE HEAT. FOLD OMELET IN HALF. TRANSFER ONTO A WARM PLATE.

SERVE 2

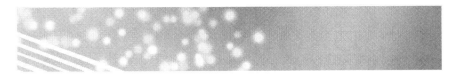

FISH

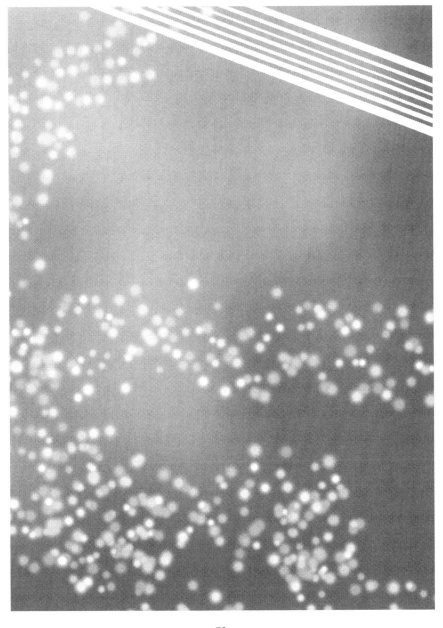

PAN-FRIED FISH

1 POUND FRESH OR FROZEN FISH FILLETS

(1/2 TO 1 INCH THICK)

1 BEATEN EGG

2/3 CUP CORNMEAL OR FINE DRY BREAD CRUMBS

SHORTENING OR COOKING OIL FOR FRYING

THAW FISH, IF FROZEN. MEASURE THICKNESS OF FISH. CUT INTO SERVING-SIZE PORTIONS. PAT DRY. IN A SHALLOW DISH COMBINE EGG AND 2 TABLESPOON WATER IN ANOTHER DISH. MIX CORNMEAL OR BREAD CRUMBS, 1/2 TEASPOON SALT AND DASH BLACK PEPPER. DIP FISH INTO EGG MIXTURE, THEN COAT WITH CORNMEAL MIXTURE.

IN A LARGE SKILLET HEAT 1/4 INCH MELTED SHORTENING OR OIL. ADD HALF OF THE FISH IN A SINGLE LAYER. (IF FILLETS HAVE SKIN, FRY SKIN SIDE LAST). FRY FISH ON ONE SIDE UNTIL GOLDEN. ALLOW 3 OR 4 MINUTES PER SIDE FOR 1/2 INCH THICK FILLETS (5 TO 6 MINUTES PER SIDE FOR 1-INCH-THICK FILLETS). TURN CAREFULLY. FRY TILL GOLDEN AND FISH FLAKES EASILY WITH A FORK. DRAIN ON PAPER TOWELS. KEEP WARM IN A 300 DEGREE OVEN WHILE FRYING REMAINING FISH. MAKES 4 SERVINGS.

CREAMED TUNA

1/4 CUP SLICED GREEN ONION

3 TABLESPOONS MARGARINE OR BUTTER

3 TABLESPOONS ALL-PURPOSE FLOUR

1-1/3 CUPS MILK

1/2 CUP DAIRY SOUR CREAM

1 9-1/4-OUNCE CAN TUNA, DRAINED

3 TABLESPOONS DRY WHITE WINE OR MILK

4 ENGLISH MUFFINS, SPLIT AND TOASTED, OR TOAST POINTS

2 TABLESPOONS SLICED ALMONDS, TOASTED

IN A SAUCEPAN COOK ONION IN MARGARINE TILL TENDER. STIR IN FLOUR, 1/4 TEASPOON SALT AND DASH PEPPER. ADD MILK ALL AT ONCE. COOK AND STIR TILL THICKENED AND BUBBLY. STIR ABOUT 1 CUP OF THE HOT MIXTURE INTO SOUR CREAM; RETURN ALL TO SAUCEPAN. GENTLY STIR IN TUNA AND WINE OR MILK. HEAT THROUGH (DO NOT BOIL). SERVE OVER MUFFIN HALVES OR TOAST POINTS. SPRINKLE WITH ALMONDS. SERVE 4

FISH BOATS

1/4 LB. BUTTER OR MARGARINE

1/2 CUP A.1. SAUCE

1/4 CUP REAL LEMON RECONSTITUTED LEMON JUICE

2 LBS. FROZEN OR FRESH FISH FILLETS

(RECOMMENDED SOLE OR FLOUNDER)

HEAVY DUTY REYNOLDS WRAP

PAPRIKA

THAW FISH FILLETS IF FROZEN. MELT BUTTER OR MARGARINE. MIX WITH A.1. SAUCE AND REAL LEMON JUICE. CUT FISH INTO SERVING-SIZE PIECES, PLACING EACH SERVING IN CENTER OF REYNOLDS WRAP, CUP FOIL AND POUR SAUCE OVER FISH. LOOSELY SEAL EDGES OF EACH "FISH BOAT". BAKE IN PRE-HEATED OVEN AT 350 DEGREES FOR ABOUT 20 MINUTES.

UNWRAP "FISH BOATS" (DON'T LOSE ANY OF THE SAUCE) SPRINKLE WITH PAPRIKA AND SERVE IN FOIL. MAKE 4 TO 6 INDIVIDUAL "FISH BOATS".

FRENCH-FRIED SHRIMP

2 POUNDS FRESH OR FROZEN SHRIMP

SHORTENING OR COOKING OIL FOR DEEP-FAT FRYING

3/4 CUP ALL-PURPOSE FLOUR

1/4 CUP YELLOW CORNMEAL

1/2 TEASPOON SUGAR

1/2 TEASPOON SALT

DASH PEPPER

1 BEATEN EGG

3/4 CUP COLD WATER

2 TABLESPOONS COOKING OIL

COCKTAIL SAUCE (FOLLOWS)

THAW SHRIMP, IF FROZEN. IN A LARGE DEEP
SAUCEPAN OR DEEP-FAT FRYER, HEAT 2 INCHES
MELTED SHORTENING OR OIL TO 375 DEGREES.
MEANWHILE, FOR BATTER, STIR TOGETHER FLOUR,
CORNMEAL, SUGAR, SALT, AND PEPPER. MAKE
A WELL IN THE CENTER. COMBINE EGG, COLD
WATER, AND THE 2 TABLESPOONS OIL; ADD TO DRY
INGREDIENTS. BEAT WITH A ROTARY BEATER TILL
SMOOTH. DIP SHRIMP INTO BATTER.

FRY SHRIMP, A FEW AT A TIME, IN THE HOT FAT FOR 2 TO 3 MINUTES OR TILL GOLDEN. REMOVE WITH A SLOTTED SPOON; DRAIN ON PAPER TOWELS. KEEP WARM IN A 300 DEGREES OVEN WHILE FRYING REMAINDER. SERVE WITH THE FOLLOWING COCKTAIL SAUCE. MAKE 5 SERVINGS.

COCKTAIL SAUCE

IN A BOWL COMBINE 3/4 CUP CHILI SAUCE; 2 TABLESPOONS LEMON JUICE; 1 TABLESPOON PREPARED HORSERADISH, 2 TEASPOONS WORCESTERSHIRE SAUCE; 1 GREEN ONION, SLICED OR 1/4 TEASPOON DRIED MINCED ONION; AND SEVERAL DASHES BOTTLED HOT PEPPER SAUCE. COVER AND STORE IN THE REFRIGERATOR UP TO 2 WEEKS. SERVE WITH SHRIMP. MAKE ABOUT 1 CUP (SIXTEEN 1 TABLESPOON SERVINGS).

LEMON FRIED PERCH

2 POUNDS PERCH FILLETS OR OTHER FISH FILLETS

1/4 CUP LEMON JUICE

3 EGGS, BEATEN

1-1/2 TEASPOON SALT

1 CUP FLOUR OR CORNMEAL

CUT FILLETS INTO SERVING-SIZE PORTIONS. PLACE FISH IN A SHALLOW BAKING DISH. POUR LEMON JUICE OVER FISH AND LET STAND 10 MINUTES, TURNING ONCE. COMBINE EGGS AND SALT. ROLL FILLETS IN FLOUR OR CORNMEAL AND DIP IN EGGS. FRY IMMEDIATELY IN HOT FAT AT MODERATE HEAT, UNTIL BROWN ON ONE SIDE; TURN CAREFULLY AND BROWN THE OTHER SIDE. COOKING TIME APPROXIMATELY 6 TO 8 MINUTES DEPENDING ON THICKNESS OF FISH. SERVE 6.

POTATO CRUSTED WHITEFISH

1 CUP LIGHT MAYONNAISE

1 TBLS DIJON-STYLE MUSTARD

1 TBLS WHOLE GRAIN MUSTARD

1 TBLS LEMON JUICE

1 TSPS LEMON ZEST CHOPPED

SALT & PEPPER (TO TASTE)

RUSSET POTATO-BAKED, COOKED & GRATED (2 EA.)

2 TBLS OLIVE OIL

8 OZ. WHITEFISH FILLETS (4 EA.)

(1) MIX MAYONNAISE, DIJON-STYLE MUSTARD, WHOLE GRAIN MUSTARD, LEMON JUICE, LEMON ZEST, SALT & PEPPER.

(2) TOSS SHREDDED POTATO WITH OLIVE OIL

(3) RUB WHITEFISH FILLETS WITH MAYONNAISE MIXTURE, TOP FILLETS WITH POTATOES & BAKE AT 425 DEGREES - 15-20 MINUTES.

SALMON LOAF

1/4 CUP FINELY CHOPPED ONION

1 TEASPOON DRIED DILL WEED

1 TABLESPOON MARGARINE OR BUTTER

1 SLIGHTLY BEATEN EGG

1 CUP SOFT BREAD CRUMBS

1/4 CUP MILK

1 15 1/2-OUNCE CAN PINK SALMON, DRAINED, FLAKED, AND SKIN AND BONES REMOVED; OR 6 1/2-OUNCE CANS TUNA, DRAINED AND BROKEN INTO CHUNKS

CHEESE SAUCE RECIPE FOLLOWS

IN A SAUCEPAN COOK ONION, DILLWEED, AND A DASH PEPPER IN MARGARINE TILL ONION IS TENDER. COMBINE EGG, BREAD CRUMBS, MILK, AND ONION MIXTURE. ADD SALMON; MIX WELL. SHAPE INTO A 6X3-INCH LOAF IN A GREASED SHALLOW BAKING PAN. BAKE IN A 350 DEGREE OVEN FOR 30 TO 35 MINUTES. TOP WITH THE FOLLOWING CHEESE SAUCE OR CHEESE SLICES, IF DESIRED. MAKE 4 SERVINGS.

CHEESE SAUCE

1 TABLESPOON MARGARINE OR BUTTER

1 TABLESPOON ALL-PURPOSE FLOUR

3/4 CUP SHREDDED PROCESS SWISS OR AMERICAN CHEESE

3/4 CUP MILK

DASH PEPPER

IN A SMALL SAUCEPAN MELT MARGARINE OR BUTTER. STIR IN FLOUR, SALT, AND PEPPER. ADD MILK ALL AT ONCE. COOK AND STIR OVER MEDIUM HEAT TILL THICKENED AND BUBBLY. ADD THE CHEESE INTO THE SAUCE TILL MELTED. COOK AND STIR 1 MINUTE MORE.

SEAFOOD STIR FRY

1 TBSP. OIL

1 PKG. LOUIS KEMP "FAT FREE FLAKE-STYLE CRAB DELIGHTS"

1-1/2 C. ORIENTAL-STYLE VEGETABLES

1/2 TSP. GARLIC POWDER

1/2 TSP. GROUND GINGER

2 TBSP. SOY SAUCE OR SEASONING PACKET FROM VEGETABLES

HEAT OIL IN SKILLET. ADD CRAB DELIGHTS AND VEGETABLES. STIR OVER MEDIUM HIGH HEAT FOR 2 MINUTES. ADD SEASONING. COOK 1 MINUTE MORE. SERVE IMMEDIATELY.

SHRIMP CREOLE

12 OUNCES FRESH OR FROZEN PEELED AND DEVEINED SHRIMP

1/2 CUP CHOPPED ONION

1/2 CUP CHOPPED CELERY

1/2 CUP GREEN PEPPER

2 CLOVES GARLIC, MINCED

2 TABLESPOONS MARGARINE OR BUTTER

1 16-OUNCE CAN TOMATOES, CUT UP

2 TABLESPOON SNIPPED PARSLEY

1/2 TEASPOON SALT

1/2 TEASPOON PAPRIKA

1/8 TO 1/4 TEASPOON GROUND RED PEPPER

1 BAY LEAF

2 TABLESPOONS COLD WATER

4 TEASPOONS CORNSTARCH

2 CUPS HOT COOKED RICE

THAW SHRIMP, IF FROZEN. IN A LARGE SKILLET COOK ONION, CELERY, GREEN PEPPER, AND GARLIC IN MARGARINE OR BUTTER TILL TENDER BUT NOT BROWN. STIR IN UNDRAINED TOMATOES, PARSLEY, SALT, PAPRIKA, RED PEPPER, AND

BAY LEAF. BRING TO BOILING, REDUCE HEAT.
COVER AND SIMMER FOR 15 MINUTES. STIR
TOGETHER COLD WATER AND CORNSTARCH.
STIR CORNSTARCH MIXTURE AND SHRIMP
INTO TOMATO MIXTURE. COOK AND STIR TILL
THICKENED AND BUBBLY. COOK AND STIR ABOUT
2 MINUTES MORE OR TILL SHRIMP TURN PINK.
REMOVE BAY LEAF. SERVE OVER RICE. MAKE 4
SERVINGS.

SALMON PATTIES

1 CAN (14-3/4) ALASKA SALMON

3/4 CUP DRY BREAD CRUMBS

1/2 CUP THINLY SLICED GREEN ONIONS

1/4 CUP CHOPPED PARSLEY

1 TEASPOON DILL WEED

2 EGGS

2 TABLESPOONS LEMON JUICE

1 TABLESPOON VEGETABLE OIL

HAMBURGER BUNS, OPTIONAL

TOMATO SLICES, OPTIONAL

DRAIN AND FLAKE SALMON, RESERVING 1/2 CUP LIQUID. MIX TOGETHER FLAKED SALMON, BREAD CRUMBS, GREEN ONIONS, PARSLEY AND DILL. MIX IN EGGS, LEMON JUICE AND RESERVED SALMON LIQUID. FORM MIXTURE INTO 4 PATTIES. HEAT OIL IN NON-STICK FRYING PAN. SAUTE-PATTIES OVER MEDIUM HEAT UNTIL GOLDEN BROWN ON BOTH SIDES. PLACE SALMON PATTIES ON HAMBURGER BUNS; GARNISH WITH LETTUCE LEAVES AND TOMATO SLICES IF DESIRED.

MAKE 4 SERVINGS.

TUNA NOODLE CASSEROLE

1 TBS. MARGARINE OR BUTTER

1 MED. ONION-CHOPPED

1 CAN CAMPBELL'S COND. CREAM OF MUSHROOM SOUP

1-1/4 CUP OF MILK

1/4 TSP. PEPPER

1/2 TSP. PREPARED MUSTARD

1 CAN-4 OZ. PIECES & STEAMS MUSHROOMS

2 CUPS-8 OZ. SHREDDED CHEESE

1-6 OZ. CAN CHICKEN OF THE SEA TUNA

1 CUP FROZEN PEAS

8 OZ. PENN DUTCH NOODLES

(COOK 6 TO 7 MINUTES, DRAIN)

1/2 CAN DURKEE FRIED ONIONS

1.IN 2 QT. SAUCEPAN, MELT MARGARINE OVER MEDIUM HEAT. ADD ONION-COOK, STIRRING 3 MINUTES. STIR IN SOUP, MILK, MUSTARD AND PEPPER. STIR CONSTANTLY-BRING TO A BOIL. REMOVE FROM HEAT.

2.STIR IN CHEESE UNTIL SMOOTH, ADD DRAINED TUNA AND PEAS. IN 2 QT. CASSEROLE, COMBINE TUNA MIXTURE & EGG NOODLES. SPRINKLE WITH FRIED ONIONS.

3.BAKE IN 350 DEGREES F OVEN FOR 25 TO 30 MINUTES OR UNTIL HEATED THROUGH.

MAKE 6 SERVINGS.

MEAT

BARBECUE-STYLE RIBS

2 SLABS PORK RIBS

1 BOT. OPEN PIT BARBECUE SAUCE

1/4 CUP VINEGAR

1/4 CUP PACKED BROWN SUGAR

1 CUP CHOPPED ONIONS

1 SMALL CLOVE GARLIC, MINCED

1/2 STICK MARGARINE OR BUTTER

PLACE RIBS ON A RACK IN THE OVEN OR ON AN OPEN BARBECUE PIT. GRILL SLOWLY ON EACH SIDE UNTIL BROWNED.

MEANWHILE, FOR SAUCE, COOK ONIONS AND GARLIC IN HOT OIL TILL TENDER IN A SAUCE PAN. ADD ALL THE REST OF THE INGREDIENTS. SIMMER FOR 15 MINUTES, STIRRING OCCASIONALLY. SPOON SAUCE ON EACH SIDE OF RIB (ONE AT A TIME) COOKING EACH SIDE SLOWLY BETWEEN EACH ADDITION. SIMMER RIBS AFTER ADDING 1/4 CUP WATER TO THE BOTTOM OF A ROASTER FOR ABOUT 30 MINUTES.

BEEF POT ROAST (SLOW COOKER)

1 BEEF CHUCK POT ROAST

(ABOUT 2-1/2 POUNDS)

1/2 CUP FLOUR

SALT AND BLACK PEPPER

3 MEDIUM BAKING POATOES, UNPEELED

(ABOUT 1 POUND)

2 LARGE CARROTS

1 LARGE PARNIP

2 LARGE CELERY STALKS

1 MEDIUM ONION, SLICED

2 BAY LEAVES

1 TEASPOON DRIED ROSEMARY

1/2 TEASPOON DRIED THYME

1/2 CUP BEEF BOUILLON

1.TRIM ANY EXCESS FAT FROM BEEF. DISCARD FAT. CUT BEEF INTO SERVING SIZE PIECES; SEASON WITH FLOUR, SALT AND PEPPER TO TASTE. BROWN BEEF IN HOT OIL.

2.SCRUB POTATOES. CUT SCRUBBED POTATOES INTO QUARTERS. CUT CARROTS AND PARNIP DIAGONALLY INTO 3/4-INCH SLICES. SLICE CELERY INTO 1-1/2- TO 2-INCH PIECES.

3.PLACE POTATOES, CARROTS, PARNIP, CELERY, ONION AND BAY LEAVES IN SLOW COOKER OR OVEN. SPRINKLE ROSEMARY AND THYME OVER VEGETABLES.

4.ARRANGE BEEF OVER VEGETABLES IN SLOW COOKER OR OVEN. POUR BROTH OVER BEEF.

5.COVER SLOW COOKER OR OVEN (350 DEGREES). COOK POT ROAST IN SLOW COOKER ON LOW ABOUT 8-1/2 TO 9 HOURS OR UNTIL BEEF IS FORK TENDER, COOK IN OVEN ABOUT 2 HOURS UNTIL FORK TENDER ALSO.

6.REMOVE BEEF TO LARGE SERVING PLATTER. ARRANGE VEGETABLES AROUND BEEF ON PLATTER. REMOVE AND DISCARD BAY LEAVES. SERVE POT ROAST WITH JUICES OR GRAVY (SHOWN BELOW)

LADLE THE JUICES FROM THE SLOW COOKER INTO A 2 CUP MEASURING CUP; PLACE IN A SMALL SAUCEPAN AND HEAT TO A BOIL. FOR EACH CUP OF JUICE, MIX 1/4 CUP OF COLD WATER AND 2 TABLESPOONS OF FLOUR UNTIL SMOOTH. ADD TO THE BOILING JUICES, STIRRING CONSTANTLY; COOK 1 MINUTES OR UNTIL THICKENED.

CHITTERLINGS

PLACE CHITTERLINGS IN WARM WATER. CUT OUT
EXCESS FAT AND SCRAPE OUT GRIT ONE AT A TIME.
WASH THROUGHLY AND PUT IN HEAVY BOILER.
ADD 3 CUPS OF WATER, 1 LARGE ONION, CUT-UP-2
GARLIC CLOVES, 2 SMALL CHOPPED RED PEPPERS,
SALT, VINEGAR, AND BLACK PEPPER TO TASTE...
COVER AND COOK ON MEDIUM HEAT UNTIL THEY
BEGIN TO STEAM. THEN REDUCE HEAT AND COOK
ON LOW FOR APPROXIMATELY 3 HOURS, STIRRING
OCCASIONALLY.

CHUCK STEAK

1 1-1/2 TO 1-3/4 POUND BEEF CHUCK STEAK, CUT 1 INCH THICK

1/4 CUP COOKING OIL

1/4 CUP CHOPPED ONION

1 TEASPOON FINELY SHREDDED LEMON PEEL

1/3 CUP LEMON JUICE

1 TABLESPOON SUGAR

1 TABLESPOON WORCESTERSHIRE SAUCE

1 TEASPOON PREPARED MUSTARD

SLASH FAT ON EDGES OF ROAST. PLACE MEAT IN A PLASTIC BAG SET IN A SHALLOW DISH. FOR MARINADE, COMBINE LEMON PEEL, LEMON JUICE COOKING OIL, ONION SUGAR, WORCESTERSIRE SAUCE, MUSTARD, 1/4 TEASPOON SALT AND 1/4 TEASPOON PEPPER. POUR OVER ROAST. SEAL BAG. MARINATE IN THE REFRIGERATOR FOR 6 TO 24 HOURS, TURNING BAG OCCASIONALLY.
REMOVE ROAST FROM BAG, RESERVING MARINADE. PLACE MEAT ON THE UNHEATED RACK OF A BOILER PAN. BROIL 3 INCHES FROM THE HEAT FOR 6 MINUTES. TURN, BRUSH WITH MARINADE, AND BROIL TO DESIRED DONENESS, ALLOWING 6 TO 8 MINUTES MORE FOR MEDIUM. BRUSH OCCASIONALLY WITH MARINADE. TO SERVE, THINLY SLICE MEAT ACROSS THE GRAIN. SERVE 6.

CITY CHICKEN

1 POUND PORK, CUT IN 1-1/2 INCH CUBES

1 POUND VEAL, CUT IN 1-1/2 INCH CUBES

2/3 CUP FINELY CRUSHED SALTINE CRACKERS (18)

1 TEASPOON PAPRIKA

3/4 TEASPOON POULTRY SEASONING

1 SLIGHTLY BEATEN EGG

2 TABLESPOONS MILK

3 TABLESPOONS SHORTENING

1 CHICKEN BOUILLON CUBE

1/2 CUP BOILING WATER

THREAD PORK AND VEAL CUBES ALTERNATELY ON 6 SKEWERS. MIX CRUMBS, PAPRIKA, POULTRY SEASONING, AND 1-1/2 TEASPOON SALT. COMBINE EGG AND MILK. DIP MEAT IN EGG MIXTURE, THEN IN CRUMBS. BROWN IN HOT SHORTENING. DISSOLVE BOUILLON CUBE IN BOILING WATER; ADD TO MEAT. BAKE, COVERED AT 350 DEGREES FOR 45 MINUTES. UNCOVER, BAKE 30 MINUTES MORE. SERVE 6.

CORNED BEEF AND VEGETABLES

1 CORNED BEEF (3 TO 5 POUND)

1 ONION, STUDDED WITH 2 WHOLE CLOVES

2 CARROTS, PEELED AND HALVED

1 RIB CELERY, HALVED

2 SPRINGS CILANTRO OR PARSLEY

1 GREEN CABBAGE (ABOUT 1 POUND CORED AND CUT INTO 6 WEDGES)

6 TO 8 SMALL NEW RED POTATOES

3 GREEN ONIONS

2 TBS. CHOPPED CILANTRO OR PARSLEY

1/2 LB. FRESH BROCCOLI

SALT AND PEPPER

REMOVE MEAT FROM PACKAGE. COOK CORNED BEEF AS DIRECTED ON PACKAGE, UNTIL FOLK TENDER, ADDING ONIONS, HALVED CARROTS, CELERY, AND CILANTRO SPRIGS. REMOVE CORNED BEEF FROM POT AND KEEP WARM. ADD CABBAGE, POTATOES, GREEN ONIONS, SALT AND PEPPER TO TASTE, AND CHOPPED CILANTRO TO LIQUID IN POT. BRING TO A BOIL, THEN REDUCE HEAT AND SIMMER, COVERED FOR 30 MINUTES OR UNTIL VEGETABLES ARE TENDER. ADD BROCCOLI DURING LAST 5 MINUTES. ARRANGE CORNED BEEF ON PLATTER WITH VEGETABLES AND BROTH.

CORNED BEEF HASH

2 TABLESPOON MARGARINE OR BUTTER

2 CUPS FINELY CHOPPED COOKED POTATOES OR LOOSE-PACK FROZEN HASH BROWN POTATOES, THAWED

1-1/2 CUPS FINELY CHOPPED COOKED CORNED BEEF OR BEEF

1/2 CUP CHOPPED ONIONS

2 TABLESPOON SNIPPED PARSLEY

1 TO 2 TEASPOONS WORCESTERSHIRE SAUCE

2 TABLESPOONS MILK, OPTIONAL

IN A LARGE SKILLET MELT MARGARINE. STIR IN POTATOES, MEAT, ONION, PARSLEY, WORCESTERSHIRE SAUCE, AND 1/8 TEASPOON PEPPER. SPREAD EVENLY INTO SKILLET. COOK OVER MEDIUM HEAT FOR 8 TO 10 MINUTES OR TILL BROWNED ON BOTTOM, TURNING OCCASIONALLY. STIR IN MILK, IF DESIRED, AND HEAT THROUGH. SERVE 4.

HAM

GLAZE

1 TABLESPOON MOLASSES

1 TABLESPOON MUSTARD

2 TABLESPOONS LIGHT BROWN SUGAR

2 TABLESPOONS DARK BROWN SUGAR

3 TABLESPOONS LIGHT CORN SYRUP

1/4 TEASPOON CINNAMON

1/4 TEASPOON NUTMEG

1/4 TEASPOON GROUND GINGER

TOPPING

WHOLE CLOVES-APPROX. 20

2 TABLESPOONS LIGHT BROWN SUGAR

2 TABLESPOONS DARK BROWN SUGAR

LINE PAN WITH ALUMINUM FOIL. PLACE HAM IN PAN, SCORE AND PLACE 20 CLOVES ON THE HAM. MELT GLAZE INGREDIENTS TOGETHER AND POUR OVER HAM. COVER HAM WITH ALUMINUM FOIL AND PLACE IN 250 DEGREE OVEN FOR APPROX. 1 HOUR. BASTE HAM 2-3 TIMES. REMOVE HAM FROM OVEN AND MIX TOGETHER AN ADDITIONAL 2 TABLESPOONS OF LIGHT BROWN SUGAR AND 2 TABLESPOON OF DARK BROWN SUGAR. PAT OVER HAM. BAKE FOR AN ADDITIONAL 20-30 MINUTES.

LONDON BROIL

1 1- TO 1-1/2 POUND BEEF FLANK STEAK; OR TOP ROUND STEAK

1/4 CUP COOKING OIL

2 TABLESPOONS VINEGAR OR LEMON JUICE

1 CLOVE GARLIC, MINCED

SCORE MEAT BY MAKING SHALLOW CUTS AT 1-INCH INTERVALS DIAGONALLY ACROSS THE STEAK IN A DIAMOND PATTERN. REPEAT ON SECOND SIDE. PLACE MEAT IN A PLASTIC BAG AND SET IN A SHALLOW DISH. FOR MARINADE, COMBINE OIL, VINEGAR, GARLIC, 1/4 TEASPOON SALT, 1/4 TEASPOON PEPPER. POUR OVER MEAT. SEAL BAG, MARINATE AT ROOM TEMPERATURE UP TO 1 HOUR OR IN REFRIGERATOR UP TO 24 HOURS; TURN BAG OCCASIONALLY.

REMOVE MEAT FROM MARINADE AND PLACE ON THE UNHEATED RACK OF A BOILER PAN. BROIL 3 INCHES FROM RACK FOR 6 MINUTES. TURN AND BROIL FOR 5 TO 6 MINUTES MORE FOR RARE OR 7 TO 8 FOR MEDIUM RARE. SEASON TO TASTE. TO SERVE, THINLY SLICE DIAGONALLY ACROSS THE GRAIN. SERVE 4 TO 6.

LIVER AND ONIONS

1 MEDIUM ONION, SLICED AND SEPARATED INTO RINGS

2 TABLESPOONS MARGARINE OR BUTTER

1 POUND SLICED BEEF LIVER

2 TEASPOONS WATER

1 TABLESPOON FLOUR

IN A LARGE SKILLET COOK ONION AND MARGARINE UNTIL TENDER BUT NOT BROWN. REMOVE FROM SKILLET. ADD LIVER AND SPRINKLE WITH SALT AND PEPPER. COOK OVER MEDIUM HEAT FOR 3 MINUTES. TURN LIVER OVER AND RETURN ONION TO SKILLET. COOK FOR 2 OR 3 MINUTES LONGER OR UNTIL LIVER IS SLIGHTLY PINK IN CENTER. REMOVE LIVER AND ONION FROM SKILLET. STIR WATER AND FLOUR INTO PAN DRIPPINGS TO MAKE GRAVY; SIMMER. POUR OVER LIVER AND ONIONS. MAKE 4 SERVINGS.

MEAT LOAF

1-1/2 LB. GROUND BEEF

1 CUP TOMATO JUICE

3/4 CUP OATS, UNCOOKED

1 EGG, BEATEN

1/4 CHOPPED ONION

1 TEASPOON SALT

1/4 TEASPOON PEPPER

1/4 CUP CHOPPED GREEN PEPPERS

PREHEAT OVEN TO 350 DEGREES F. COMBINE
ALL INGREDIENTS; MIX WELL. PRESS FIRMLY INTO
UNGREASED 8X4X2-INCH LOAF PAN. BAKE 350
DEGREES F ABOUT 1 HOUR. LET STAND 5 MINUTES
BEFORE SLICING. MAKE 8 SERVINGS.

PEPPER STEAK

1-1/2 POUNDS SIRLOIN STEAK, 1/2-INCH THICK

1/2 TEASPOON SALT

2 MEDIUM ONIONS, CHOPPED (1 CUP)

1 CUP BEEF BROTH

3 TABLESPOONS SOY SAUCE

1 CLOVE GARLIC, MINCED

2 GREEN PEPEPRS, CUT INTO STRIPS

2 TABLESPOONS CORNSTARCH

1/4 CUP COLD WATER

3 TO 4 CUPS HOT COOKED RICE

TRIM FAT AND BONE FROM MEAT; CUT INTO STRIPS. GREASE LARGE SKILLET LIGHTLY WITH THE FAT FROM MEAT. BROWN MEAT THOROUGHLY ON ONE SIDE; TURN AND SEASON WITH ONE-QUARTER TEASPOON SALT. BROWN OTHER SIDE OF MEAT; TURN AND SEASON WITH REMAINING, ONE-QUARTER TEASPOON SALT. PUSH MEAT TO ONE SECTION. ADD ONION, COOK AND STIR UNTIL TENDER. STIR IN BROTH, SOY SAUCE, AND GARLIC. COVER AND SIMMER 10 MINUTES OR UNTIL MEAT IS TENDER. ADD GREEN PEPPER STRIPS. COVER AND SIMMER FIVE MINUTES. BLEND CORNSTARCH

AND WATER; STIR GRADUALLY INTO MEAT
MIXTURE. COOK, STIRRING CONSTANTLY UNTIL
MIXTURE THICKENS AND BOILS. BOIL AND STIR
FOR ONE MINUTE. SERVE WITH COOKED RICE.

PORK CHOPS

2 TABLESPOONS SHORTENING

6 MEDIUM PORK CHOPS

FLOUR

SALT AND PEPPER TO TASTE

2 TABLESPOONS FLOUR

1 CUP WATER

PREHEAT OVEN TO 350 DEGREES. MELT
SHORTENING IN FRYING PAN. ROLL CHOPS IN
FLOUR AND BROWN ON BOTH SIDES. REMOVE
TO DEEP BAKING DISH. SEASON WITH SALT AND
PEPPER. STIR TOGETHER 2 TABLESPOONS FLOUR
AND WATER UNTIL WELL COMBINED. ADD TO
SAME FRYING PAN AND STIR, SCRAPING UP PAN
DRIPPINGS, OVER MEDIUM HEAT UNTIL THICK.
POUR OVER CHOPS. BAKE 50 TO 60 MINUTES OR
UNTIL CHOPS ARE TENDER. SERVE 3 TO 4.

REUBEN SANDWICHES

8 SLICES DARK RYE OR PUMPERNICKEL BREAD

3 TABLESPOONS MARGARINE OR BUTTER, SOFTENED

1/4 CUP THOUSAND ISLAND OR RUSSIAN SALAD DRESSING

1/2 POUND THINLY SLICED COOKED CORNED BEEF, PORK, OR HAM

4 SLICES SWISS CHEESE (1-1/2 OUNCES)

1 CUP SAUERKRAUT, WELL DRAINED

SPREAD ONE SIDE OF EACH SIDE OF BREAD WITH MARGARINE AND THE OTHER SIDE WITH SALAD DRESSING. WITH THE MARGARINE SIDE DOWN, TOP FOUR SLICES OF BREAD WITH MEAT, CHEESE AND SAUERKRAUT. TOP WITH REMAINING BREAD SLICES, DRESING SIDE DOWN. IN A LARGE SKILLET COOK 2 SANDWICHES OVER MEDIUM HEAT FOR 4 TO 6 MINUTES OR TILL BREAD TOAST AND CHEESE MELTS, TURNING ONCE. REPEAT WITH REMAINING SANDWICHES. MAKE 4 SERVINGS.

SHORT RIBS

1 LARGE ONION, CHOPPED

3/4 CUP KETCHUP

3 TABLESPOONS RED WINE

2 TABLESPOONS WORCESTERSHIRE SAUCE

1-1/2 TABLESPOONS BROWN SUGAR

1-1/2 TEASPOONS PREPARED MUSTARD

2 TEASPOONS CHILI POWDER

1-1/2 TEASPOON SALT

1/4 TEASPOON PEPPER

3 LB. SHORT RIBS

2 TABLESPOONS VEGETABLE OIL

1-1/4 CUP WATER

1 TABLESPOON FLOUR

COOK SHORT RIBS IN PRESSURE COOKER

PRESSURE COOKING TIME: 30 MINUTES

YIELD: 5 SERVINGS

1.IN A BOWL, COMBINE ALL INGREDIENTS EXCEPT RIBS, OIL, ONION, WATER AND FLOUR. ADD RIBS. MIX WELL AND MARINATE OVERNIGHT IN THE REFRIGERATOR FOR AT LEAST 4 HOURS.

2.DIVIDE THE RIBS INTO TWO BATCHES. RESERVE MARINADE. HEAT OIL IN COOKER FOR ABOUT 2 MINUTES. BROWN EACH BATCH ON ALL SIDES AND REMOVE.

3.TO THE REMAINING OIL IN COOKER, ADD ONION. STIR FRY TILL ONION IS TRANSPARENT. ADD RIBS, MARINADE AND 1 CUP OF WATER. STIR.

4.CLOSE COOKER. BRING TO FULL PRESSURE ON HIGH HEAT. REDUCE HEAT AND COOK FOR 30 MINUTES.

5.REMOVE COOKER FROM HEAT, ALLOW TO COOL.

6.OPEN COOKER. PLACE SHORT RIBS ON SERVING DISH. KEEP HOT.

7.DRAIN OFF FAT FROM COOKING LIQUID. IN A SEPARATE BOWL, GRADUALLY ADD REMAINING INGREDIENTS (1/4 CUP) TO FLOUR, BLENDING UNTIL SMOOTH. USING A WIRE WHISK, GRADUALLY ADD THIS MIXTURE TO LIQUID IN COOKER. PLACE COOKER ON MEDIUM HEAT. COOK UNTIL SAUCE THICKENS. STIRRING CONSTANTLY. POUR SAUCE OVER MEAT. SERVE HOT.

SPAGHETTI

1 POUND GROUND BEEF OR GROUND PORK

1-1/2 CUPS SLICED FRESH MUSHROOMS

1/2 CUP CHOPPED ONION

1/2 CHOPPED GREEN PEPPER

2 CLOVES GARLIC, MINCED

2 16-OUNCE CANS TOMATOES, CUT UP

1 6-OUNCE CAN TOMATO PASTE

1 TEASPOONS SUGAR

1 TEASPOON DRIED OREGANO, CRUSHED

1 TEASPOON DRIED BASIL, CRUSHED

1/2 TEASPOON DRIED THYME, CRUSHED

1 BAY LEAF

6 CUPS HOT COOKED SPAGHETTI

IN A DUTCH OVEN COOK MEAT, MUSHROOMS,
ONION, GREEN PEPPER, AND GARLIC TILL MEAT
IS BROWN. DRAIN FAT. STIR IN UNDRAINED
TOMATOES, TOMATO PASTE, SUGAR, OREGANO,
BASIL, THYME, BAY LEAF, 1/2 TEASPOON SALT,
AND 1/4 TEASPOON PEPPER. BRING TO BOILING;
REDUCE HEAT. COVER; SIMMER 30 MINUTES.
UNCOVER; SIMMER 10 TO 15 MINUTES MORE OR TO

DESIRED CONSISTENCY, STIRRING OCCASIONALLY. DISCARD BAY LEAF. SERVE OVER SPAGHETTI. IF DESIRED, SPRINKLE GRATED PARMESAN CHEESE ON TOP. MAKE 6 SERVINGS.

SLOPPY JOES

(THE WAY WOOLWORTH'S LUNCH COUNTER SERVED IT 20 YEARS AGO)

IN JUST ENOUGH OIL TO COVER BOTTOM OF MEDIUM SKILLET, BROWN 2 POUNDS GROUND ROUND AND STIR WITH A FORK UNTIL ALL OF THE PINK COLOR DISAPPEARS. ON MEDIUM HEAT, STIR INTO THE BEEF:

2 ENVELOPES ONION SOUP MIX

2 CANS (10 OUNCE EACH) TOMATO SOUP

1 TABLESPOON A-1 SAUCE

1 TEASPOON WORCESTERSHIRE SAUCE

1 TEASPOON LEMON JUICE

A FEW DROPS TABASCO SAUCE

A DAB OF PREPARED YELLOW MUSTARD

3 TABLESPOONS BROWN SUGAR

STIR WELL TO COMBINE. COOK ON MEDIUM-LOW HEAT UNTIL IT COMES TO SERVING TEMPERATURE. SPOON INTO SPLIT HAMBURGER BUNS.

LEFTOVERS FREEZE WELL FOR MONTHS. MAKES ABOUT 8 TO 10 SANDWICHES.

STUFFED GREEN PEPPERS

2 LARGE GREEN PEPPERS

1/2 TEASPOON DRIED BASIL OR DRIED IREGANO, CRUSHED

3/4 POUND BEEF, GROUND PORK, GROUND LAMB OR BULK PORK SAUSAGE

1/3 CUP CHOPPED ONION

1-7-1/2 OUNCE CAN TOMATOES, CUT UP

1/3 CUP LONG GRAIN RICE

1 TABLESPOON WORCESTERSHIRE SAUCE

1/2 CUP SHREDDED AMERICAN CHEESE (2 OUNCES)

OVEN 375 DEGREES

HAVE PEPPERS LENGTHWISE, REMOVING STEM ENDS, SEEDS, AND MEMBRANES. IMMERSE PEPPERS INTO BOILING WATER FOR 3 MINUTES. SPRINKLE INSIDES WITH SALT. INVERT ON PAPER TOWELS TO DRAIN WELL. IN A SKILLET COOK MEAT AND ONION TILL MEAT IS BROWN AND ONION IS TENDER. DRAIN FAT. STIR IN UNDRAINED TOMATOES, UNCOOKED RICE, WORCESTERSHIRE, BASIL, 1/2 CUP WATER, 1/4 TEASPOON PEPPER, AND 1/4 TEASPOON SALT. BRING TO BOILING; REDUCE HEAT. COVER AND SIMMER FOR 15 TO 18 MINUTES OR TILL RICE IS TENDER. STIR IN 1/4 CUP

OF THE CHEESE. FILL PEPPERS WITH MEAT MIXTURE. PLACE IN AN 8X8X2-INCH BAKING DISH WITH ANY REMAINING MEAT MIXTURE.

BAKE IN A 375 DEGREE OVEN ABOUT 15 MINUTES OR TILL HEATED THROUGH. SPRINKLE WITH REMAINING CHEESE. LET STAND 1 TO 2 MINUTES. MAKE 4 SERVINGS.

SWEDISH MEATBALLS

1 BEATEN EGG

2-1/4 CUPS MILK OR LIGHT CREAM

3/4 CUP SOFT BREAD CRUMBS (1 SLICE)

1/2 CUP FINELY CHOPPED ONION

1/4 CUP SNIPPED PARSLEY

1/4 TEASPOON PEPPER

1/8 TEASPOON GROUND ALLSPICE OR GROUND NUTMEG

1/2 POUND GROUND BEEF OR GROUND VEAL

1/2 POUND GROUND PORK OR GROUND LAMB

1 TABLESPOON MARGARINE OR BUTTER

2 TABLESPOONS ALL-PURPOSE FLOUR

2 TEASPOONS INSTANT BEEF BOUILLON GRANULES

1/8 TEASPOON PEPPER

2 TO 3 CUPS HOT COOKED NOODLES

IN A MIXING BOWL COMBINE EGG, 1/4 CUP OF THE MILK, THE BREAD CRUMBS, ONION, PARSLEY, THE 1/4 TEASPOON PEPPER, AND THE ALLSPICE OR NUTMEG. ADD MEAT; MIX WELL. SHAPE INTO 30 MEATBALLS. IN A LARGE SKILLET COOK MEATBALLS IN MARGARINE OR BUTTER, HALF AT A TIME, OVER MEDIUM HEAT ABOUT 10 MINUTES OR TILL

NO PINK REMAINS, TURNING TO BROWN EVENLY. REMOVE MEATBALLS FROM SKILLET, RESERVING 2 TABLESPOONS DRIPPINGS. DRAIN MEATBALLS ON PAPER TOWELS. STIR FLOUR, BOUILLON GRANULES, AND THE 1/8 TEASPOON PEPPER INTO RESERVED DRIPPINGS. ADD REMAINING MILK. COOK AND STIR TILL THICKENED AND BUBBLY. COOK AND STIR 1 MINUTES MORE. RETURN MEATBALLS TO SKILLET. HEAT THROUGH. SERVE WITH NOODLES. MAKE 4 TO 6 SERVINGS.

SWEET-AND-SOUR PORK

1 8-OUNCE CAN PINEAPPLE CHUNKS (JUICE PACK)

1/3 CUP SUGAR

1/4 CUP VINEGAR

2 TABLESPOONS CORNSTARCH

2 TABLESPOONS SOY SAUCE

1 TEASPOON INSTANT CHICKEN BOUILLON GRANULES

1 BEATEN EGG

1/4 CUP CORNSTARCH

1/4 CUP ALL-PURPOSE FLOUR

1/4 CUP WATER

1/8 TEASPOON GROUND RED OR BLACK PEPPER

1 POUND BONELESS PORK, CUT INTO 3/4-INCH CUBES

SHORTENING OR COOKING OIL FOR DEEP-FAT FRYING

1 TABLESPOON COOKING OIL

2 MEDIUM CARROTS, THINLY BIAS SLICED

2 CLOVES GARLIC, MINCED

1 LARGE GREEN OR SWEET RED PEPPER, CUT INTO 1/2-INCH PIECES

2 CUPS HOT COOKED RICE

FOR SAUCE DRAIN PINEAPPLE, RESERVING JUICE. ADD WATER TO RESERVED JUICE TO EQUAL 1-1/2 CUPS. STIR IN SUGAR, VINEGAR, THE 2 TABLESPOON CORNSTARCH, THE SOY SAUSE, AND BOUILLON GRANULES, SET SAUCE ASIDE. FOR BATTER, IN A BOWL COMBINE EGG, THE 1/4 CUP CORNSTARCH, THE FLOUR, WATER, AND PEPPER. STIR TILL SMOOTH. DIP PORK CUBES INTO BATTER. FRY ONE-THIRD AT A TIME IN THE HOT SHORTENING OR OIL (365 DEGREES) FOR 4 TO 5 MINUTES OR TILL PORK IS NO LONGER PINK AND BATTER IS GOLDEN. DRAIN ON PAPER TOWELS. PREHEAT A WOK OR LARGE SKILLET OVER HIGH HEAT; ADD THE 1 TABLESPOON OIL. (ADD MORE OIL AS NECESSARY DURING COOKING.) STIR FRY CARROTS AND GARLIC IN HOT OIL FOR 1 MINUTE. ADD SWEET PEPPER; STIR FRY FOR 1 TO 2 MINUTES OR TILL CRISP-TENDER. PUSH FROM CENTER OF WOK. STIR SAUCE AND POUR INTO CENTER OF WOK. COOK AND STIR TILL THICKENED. COOK AND STIR 1 MINUTE MORE. STIR IN PORK AND PINEAPPLE. STIR TOGETHER ALL INGREDIENTS. HEAT. SERVE OVER RICE. SERVE 4.

SWISS STEAK

2 TABLESPOONS FLOUR

1/4 TEASPOON SALT

1/8 TEASPOON PEPPER

1-1/2 POUNDS BEEF BONE-IN ROUND STEAK

1 TABLESPOON SHORTENING

1 CAN (8 OUNCES) WHOLE TOMATOES

1 MEDIUM ONION, CHOPPED (ABOUT 1/2 CUP)

1/2 SMALL GREEN PEPPER, FINELY CHOPPED

1/2 TEASPOON SALT

1/8 TEASPOON PEPPER

MIX FLOUR, 1/4 TEASPOON SALT AND 1/8 TEASPOON PEPPER. SPRINKLE 1 SIDE OF BEEF STEAK WITH HALF OF THE FLOUR MIXTURE; POUND IN. TURN BEEF AND POUND IN REMAINING FLOUR MIXTURE. CUT BEEF INTO 4 OR 5 SERVING PIECES. HEAT SHORTENING IN 10-INCH SKILLET UNTIL MELTED. COOK BEEF OVER MEDIUM HEAT UNTIL BROWN, ABOUT 15 MINUTES. MIX TOMATOES (WITH LIQUID) AND REMAINING INGREDIENTS; POUR ON BEEF, HEAT TO BOILING; REDUCE HEAT. COVER AND SIMMER UNTIL BEEF IS TENDER, ABOUT 45 MINUTES.

MAKE 4 OR 5 SERVINGS.

TACOS

12 TACO SHELLS

1 POUND GROUND BEEF OR GROUND PORK

1/2 CUP CHOPPED ONION

2 CLOVES GARLIC, MINCED

1 4-OUNCE CAN DICED GREEN CHILI PEPPERS, DRAINED

1 TO 2 TEASPOONS CHILI POWDER

SEVERAL DASHES BOTTLED HOT PEPPER SAUCE (OPTIONAL)

1-1/2 CUPS SHREDDED LETTUCE

1 CUP CHOPPED TOMATOES

1 CUP SHREDDED SHARP CHEDDAR OR MONTEREY JACK CHEESE.

OVEN 350 DEGREES

HEAT TACO SHELLS ACCORDING TO PACKAGE DIRECTIONS. FOR FILLING, IN A LARGE SKILLET COOK MEAT, ONION, AND GARLIC TILL MEAT IS BROWN AND ONION IS TENDER. DRAIN FAT. STIR IN CHILI PEPPERS; CHILI POWDER; HOT PEPPER SAUCE, IF DESIRED; AND 1/4 TEASPOON SALT. HEAT THROUGH. FILL EACH TACO SHELL WITH SOME OF THE MEAT MIXTURE. TOP WITH LETTUCE, TOMATOES, AND CHEESE. IF DESIRED, SERVE WITH TACO SAUCE, SOUR CREAM, AND GUACAMOLE. MAKE 4 SERVINGS.

PASTA, RICE AND GRAINS

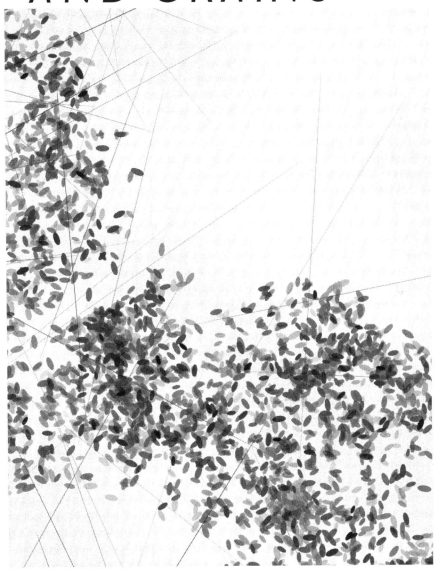

GRANOLA

2 CUPS REGULAR ROLLED OATS

1/2 CUP COCONUT

1/2 CUP COARSELY CHOPPED SLIVERED OR SLICED ALMONDS, OR CHOPPED PEANUTS

1/2 CUP SUNFLOWER NUTS

1/4 CUP SESAME SEED

1/2 CUP HONEY OR MAPLE-FLAVORED SYRUP

1/3 CUP COOKING OIL

OVEN 300 DEGREES

IN A BOWL STIR TOGETHER ROLLED OATS, COCONUT, ALMONDS OR PEANUTS, SUNFLOWER NUTS, AND SESAME SEED. IN ANOTHER BOWL COMBINE HONEY OR SYRUP AND OIL; STIR INTO OAT MIXTURE. SPREAD MIXTURE EVENLY INTO A GREASED 15X10X1-INCH BAKING PAN. BAKE IN A 300 DEGREE OVEN FOR 30 TO 35 MINUTES OR TILL LIGHTLY BROWNED, STIRRING AFTER 20 MINUTES.

REMOVE FROM THE OVEN AND IMMEDIATELY TURN OUT ONTO A LARGE PIECE OF FOIL. COOL, THEN BREAK INTO CLUMPS. STORE IN TIGHTLY COVERED JARS OR PLASTIC BAGS AT ROOM TEMPERATURE

FOR UP TO 2 WEEKS. FOR LONGER STORAGE, SEAL
IN FREEZER BAGS AND FREEZE. MAKE ABOUT 6
CUPS (12 SERVINGS)

FRIED RICE

2 TABLESPOONS COOKING OIL

2 BEATEN EGGS

1/2 CUP DICED FULLY COOKED HAM

1/4 CUP FINELY CHOPPED FRESH MUSHROOMS

1/4 CUP THINLY SLICED GREEN ONIONS

1/2 TO 1 TEASPOON GRATED GINGERROOT

DASH GROUND RED PEPPER

3 CUPS UNSLATED COOKED RICE, CHILLED

2 CUPS CHOPPED CHINESE CABBAGE

2 TABLESPOONS SOY SAUCE

IN A LARGE SKILLET HEAT 1 TABLESPOON OF THE OIL OVER MEDIUM HEAT. ADD EGGS AND COOK WITHOUT STIRRING TILL SET. LOOSEN EGGS AND INVERT SKILLET OVER CUTTING BOARD TO REMOVE, CUT INTO SHORT, NARROW STRIPS.

IN THE SKILLET HEAT THE REMAINING OIL OVER MEDIUM HEAT. COOK HAM, MUSHROOMS, ONION, GINGERROOT, AND RED PEPPEER IN THE HOT OIL FOR 3 MINUTES. STIR IN COOKED RICE, CABBAGE AND EGG STRIPS; SPRINKLE WITH SOY SAUCE AND 1 TABLESPOON WATER. COOK FOR 3 TO 5 MINUTES OR TILL HEATED THROUGH, TOSSING GENTLY TO COAT WITH SOY SAUCE. SERVE 4.

MANICOTTI

1-8 OZ. PKG. MANICOTTI NOODLES

2 TBSP. BUTTER

1/2 ONION FINELY CHOPPED

1 CLOVE GARLIC CRUSHED

1-1O OZ. PKG. FROZEN CHOPPED SPINACH DEFROSTED-

SQUEEZED DRY & CHOPPED AGAIN

1 LB. GROUND ROUND

1/4 CUP PARMESAN CHEESE GRATED

2 EGGS, LIGHTLY BEATEN

1/2 TSP. SALT

DASH PEPPER

1 LG. CAN TOMATO SAUCE

1/2 CUP SOFT BREAD CRUMBS

1/2 TSP. BASIL

COOK NOODLES FOLLOWING PKG. DIRECTIONS,
LIFT WITH SLOTTED SPOON, PLACE IN BOWL OF
COLD WATER UNTIL READY TO USE. SAUTE ONION
& GARLIC IN BUTTER. ADD SPINACH, HEAT UNTIL
MOISTURE IS ABSORBED. TRANSFER TO LARGE
BOWL. BROWN BEEF, STIR TO BREAK UP. ADD
TO SPINACH MIXTURE WITH BREAD CRUMBS,

PARMESAN CHEESE, EGGS, BASIL, SALT & PEPPER. BLEND WELL. DRAIN NOODLES ONE AT A TIME. FILL EACH WITH MEAT MIXTURE. POUR A LITTLE TOMATO SAUCE IN SHALLOW BAKING DISH. LAY MANICOTTI SIDE BY SIDE IN SAUCE. TOP WITH REMAINING SAUCE. SPRINKLE WITH PARMESAN CHEESE. BAKE UNCOVERED AT 350 DEGREES FOR 20 MIN.

POTLUCK PASTA

2 CUPS LARGE SHELLS, ROTINI, OR ELBOW MACARONI

1 10-OUNCE PACKAGE FROZEN CHOPPED BROCCOLI, PEASE, OR MIXED VEGETABLES

1/3 CUP CHOPPED ONION

1 10-3/4-OUNCE CAN CONDENSED CREAM OF CELERY, CHICKEN, OR MUSHROOM SOUP; OR ONE 11-OUNCE CAN CONDENSED CHEDDAR CHEESE SOUP

1 8-OUNCE CARTON DAIRY SOUR CREAM

1 4-OUNCE CAN MUSHROOM STEMS AND PIECES, DRAINED

1/2 CUP MILK

1/2 CUP SHREDDED CARROT

1 TEASPOON DRIED OREGAN OR BASIL, CRUSHED, OR DRIED DILLWEED

1/4 TEASPOON PEPPER

2 TEASPOONS GRATED PARMESAN CHEESE

IN A LARGE SAUCEPAN COOK PASTA, ADDING FROZEN VEGETABLE AND ONION THE LAST 6 MINUTES. DRAIN IN A COLANDER.

IN THE SAME SAUCEPAN STIR TOGETHER CONDENSED SOUP; SOUR CREAM; MUSHROOMS; MILK; CARROT; OREGANO, BASIL, OR DILLWEED; AND PEPPER. COOK AND STIR OVER MEDIUM HEAT TILL HEATED THROUGH.

STIR IN DRAINED PASTA MIXTURE; HEAT THROUGH. TRANSFER TO A WARM SERVING DISH. SPRINKLE WITH PARMESAN CHEESE AND SERVE IMMEDIATELY. MAKES 10 SERVINGS.

SHRIMP AND BROCCOLI WITH RICE

1/2 CUP LONG GRAIN WHITE RICE

1 CUP WATER

1/2 POUND UNCOOKED SHRIMP

1-1/2 CUPS BROCCOLI FLORETS

1 TABLESPOON UNSALTED BUTTER

2 GREEN ONIONS; SLICED

2 TABLESPOONS SLIVERED ALMONDS

1/2 TEASPOON CURRY POWDER

1 TEASPOON FRESHLY GRATED GINGER OR ONE-QUARTER TEASPOON GROUND GINGER

PINCH CAYENNE PEPPER

3/4 CUP HALF-AND-HALF

1/4 TEASPOON SALT

1 TEASPOON LEMON JUICE

BRING WATER TO A BOIL; ADD RICE. REDUCE HEAT TO SIMMER, COVER AND COOK 15-20 MINUTES, OR UNTIL DONE. LEAVE COVERED UNTIL SHRIMP ARE COOKED. SHELL AND DEVEIN THE SHRIMP; SET ASIDE.

CUT UP BROCCOLI, PLACE IN COVERED MICROWAVE-SAFE DISH WITH 2 TABLESPOONS

WATER. BLANCH IN MICROWAVE FOR 1-1/2 TO TWO
MINUTES; DRAIN AND SET ASIDE. MELT BUTTER
IN 10-INCH SKILLET. ADD SHRIMP AND COOK 30
SECONDS.

ADD BROCCOLI, ONIONS AND ALMONDS AND
CONTINUE COOKING FOR 90 SECONDS. SPRINKLE
WITH CURRY POWDER, GINGER AND CAYENNE
PEPPER. STIR IN HALF-AND-HALF, SALT AND LEMON
JUICE.

COOK OVER MEDIUM-HIGH HEAT UNTIL SHRIMP
ARE COOKED THROUGH, BUT NOT OVERCOOKED,
AND SAUCE HAS THICKENED SLIGHTLY. SERVE
IMMEDIATELY OVER COOKED RICE.

SPANISH RICE

1/2 CUP CHOPPED ONION

1/2 CUP CHOPPED GREEN PEPPER

1 CLOVE GARLIC, MINCED

1 TABLESPOON COOKING OIL

1 28-OUNCE CAN TOMATOES, CUT UP

3/4 CUP LONG GRAIN RICE

1 TEASPOON SUGAR

1 TEASPOON CHILI POWDER

1/4 TEASPOON SALT

1/8 TEASPOON PEPPER

SEVERAL DASHES BOTTLED HOT PEPPER SAUCE

1/2 CUP SHREDDED CHEDDAR CHEESE

(2 OUNCES) (OPTIONAL)

IN A LARGE SKILLET COOK ONION, GREEN PEPPER, SALT AND GARLIC TILL TENDER BUT NOT BROWN. STIR IN UNDRAINED TOMATOES, RICE, SUGAR, CHILI POWDER, PEPPER, HOT PEPPER SAUCE, AND 1 CUP WATER. BRING TO BOILING; REDUCE HEAT. COVER AND SIMMER FOR 20 TO 25 MINUTES OR TILL RICE IS TENDER AND MOST OF THE LIQUID IS ABSORBED. SPRINKLE WITH SHREDDED CHEDDAR CHEESE, IF DESIRED. MAKES 6 TO 8 SERVINGS.

TOFU FRIED RICE

THE RICE FOR THIS IS BEST PREPARED AND CHILLED BEFORE USING IN FRIED RICE. IN THIS WEATHER MAKE RICE WITH DINNER ONE NIGHT, THEN STICK THE COVERED PAN ON THE UNHEATED BACK PORCH OUTSIDE THE KITCHEN, WHERE IT STAYS WELL-CHILLED UNTIL DINNER THE NEXT NIGHT.

FOR THE TOFU:

1 POUND EXTRA-FIRM TOFU

1 TABLESPOON SOY SAUCE

1 TEASPOON TOASTED SESAME OIL

1/4 TO 1/2 CUP CORNSTARCH

FOR THE FRIED RICE:

4 TABLESPOONS VEGETABLE OIL

1 CUP FROZEN CHOPPED ONIONS

2 TEASPOONS MINCED GARLIC (ABOUT 4 CLOVES)

1/4 TEASPOON CRUSHED RED PEPPER FLAKES

8 OUNCES BROCCOLI SLAW

4 CUPS COOKED WHITE RICE, PREFERABLY COLD

DRAIN TOFU. SLICE IT IN HALF HORIZONTALLY TO CREATE TWO THIN SLABS. PLACE IT BETWEEN CLEAN, FOLDED CLOTH DISH TOWELS. THE TOWELS SHOULD BE FOLDED TO JUST ABOUT THE SIZE OF THE TWO TOFU PIECES LAID SIDE BY SIDE. PUT A HEAVY WEIGHT ON TOP OF THE STACK (A SKILLET WITH HEAVY CANS IN IT). SET ASIDE FOR AT LEAST 10 MINUTES (AND UP TO SEVERAL HOURS). CUT THE TOFU INTO 1/2 INCH (OR SO) SQUARES AND PUT IN A BOWL. DRIZZLE SOY SAUCE AND SESAME OIL OVER TOFU. STIR THE SQUARES GENTLY TO ALLOW THE SEASONINGS TO SOAK IN. SPRINKLE WITH 1/4 CUP CORNSTARCH. STIR GENTLY TO COAT ALL PIECES OF TOFU. SPRINKLE IN MORE IF NECESSARY, AND SET ASIDE.

SET A WOK OR WIDE, HEAVY SKILLET OVER HIGH HEAT. ADD TWO TABLESPOON OIL. WHEN IT IS VERY HOT, ADD ONIONS.

LET ONIONS COOK, STIRRING JUST A FEW TIMES, FOR ABOUT FOUR MINUTES, OR UNTIL THEY ARE FAIRLY BROWN (FRESH ONIONS WILL TAKE A LITTLE LONGER). ADD GARLIC, STIR A FEW TIMES, THEN ADD RED PEPPER FLAKES AND BROCCOLI SLAW. STIR FOR TWO MINUTES, THEN SCRAPE ONTO A LARGE PLATE. (SEE NEXT PAGE).

HEAT REMAINING TWO TABLESPOON OF OIL OVER HIGH HEAT. WHEN IT IS VERY HOT, ADD TOFU. STIRRING OCCASIONALLY, BROWN TOFU ALL OVER.

CRUMBLE RICE OVER TOFU, THEN ADD SLAW MIX AND TWO OR THREE TABLESPOON OF WATER. STIR OVER HIGH HEAT UNTIL RICE SOFTENS AND HEAT THROUGH, THEN SEASON WITH MORE SOY SAUCE AND SESAME OIL.

SERVE FOUR.

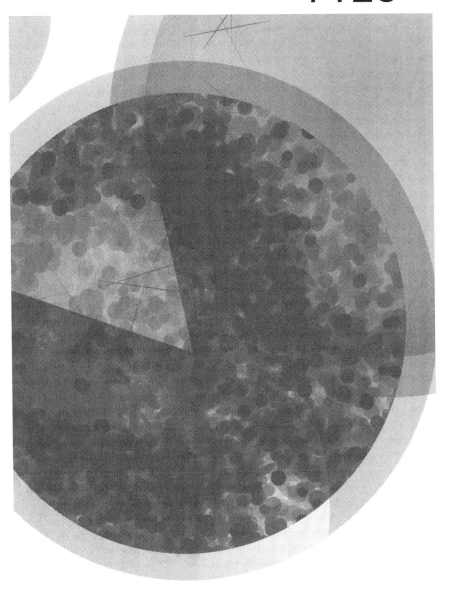

PIES

APPLE PIE

FILLING AND GLAZE:

6 CUPS SLICED, PEELED JONATHAN APPLES

(ABOUT 2 POUNDS OR 6 MEDIUM)

2 TABLESPOONS ORANGE JUICE

1/3 CUP FIRMLY PACKED LIGHT BROWN SUGAR

1/3 CUP GRANULATED SUGAR

1 TEASPOON CINNAMON

1/2 TABLESPOON ALL-PURPOSE FLOUR

1 TEASPOON CINNAMON

1/4 TEASPOON SALT

1/4 TEASPOON NUTMEG

2 TABLESPOONS BUTTER OR MARGARINE

1 TO 2 TEASPOON MILK

1 TEASPOON GRANULATED SUGAR

CRUST:

2 CUPS ALL-PURPOSE FLOUR

1 TEASPOON SALT

3/4 CUP (3/4 STICK) BUTTER FLAVOR SHORTENING

5 TABLESPOONS COLD WATER

1.HEAT OVEN TO 400 DEGREES F.

2.PREPARE BOTTOM CRUST (BELOW)

3.TOSS APPLES AND ORANGE JUICE IN LARGE BOWL. COMBINE LIGHT BROWN SUGAR, GRANULATED SUGAR, FLOUR, CINNAMON, SALT, AND NUTMEG. TOSS WITH APPLES UNTIL COATED. SPOON INTO UNBAKED PIE SHELL.

4.PREPARE TOP CRUST (BELOW)

5.BRUSH TOP WITH MILK. SPRINKLE WITH SUGAR. COVER TOP WITH SHEET OF FOIL TO PREVENT OVERBROWNING.

6.BAKE AT 400 DEGREES F FOR 40 MINUTES. REMOVE FOIL. BAKE 10 TO 20 MINUTES LONGER OR UNTIL APPLES ARE TENDER, FILLING IN CENTER IS BUBBLY, AND CRUST IS GOLDEN BROWN. COOK PIE TO ROOM TEMPERTURE BEFORE SERVING,

(CRUST ON NEXT PAGE)

CRUST

1.COMBINE FLOUR AND SALT IN MEDIUM BOWL. CUT IN CRISCO USING PASTRY BLENDER (OR 2 KNIVES) UNTIL ALL FLOUR IS JUST BLENDED IN TO FORM PEA-SIZE CHUNKS.

2.SPRINKLE WITH WATER, ONE TABLESPOON AT A TIME. TOSS LIGHTLY WITH FORK UNTIL DOUGH FORMS A BALL. DIVIDE DOUGH INTO TWO EQUAL PARTS. PRESS BETWEEN HANDS TO FORM TWO 5- TO 6-INCH PANCAKES.

3.FLOUR "PANCAKES" LIGHTLY ON BOTH SIDES. ROLL BOTTOM CRUST BETWEEN SHEETS OF WAXED PAPER (OR PLASTIC WRAP) ON DAMPED COUNTERTOP.

4.PEEL OFF TOP TOP SHEET. TRIM ONE INCH LARGER THAN UPSIDE-DOWN 9-INCH PIE PLATE. FLIP INTO PIE PLATE. REMOVE OTHER SHEET. TRIM EDGE EVEN WITH PIE PLATE.

5.ROLL TOP CRUST SAME AS BOTTOM. PEEL OFF TOP SHEET. FLIP ONTO FILLED PIE. REMOVE OTHER SHEET. TRIM 1/2 INCH BEYOND EDGE OF PIE PLATE. FOLD TOP EDGE UNDER BOTTOM CRUST. FLUTE. CUT SLITS IN TOP CRUST FOR ESCAPE OF STEAM.

MAKE ONE 9-INCH PIE

BEAN PIE

1 POUND NAVY BEANS

2-1/2 CUPS SUGAR

2 CANS EVAPORATED MILK

2 STICKS BUTTER

1 TABLESPOON FLOUR

6 EGGS

1 TEASPOON CINNAMON

1 TEASPOON VANILLA

RAW CRUST PASTRY (UNCOOKED)

COOK BEANS WELL, 1-1/2 HOURS...STRAIN BEANS
(MAKE 2 CUPS)...MIX BUTTER, SUGAR, EGGS,
MILK, AND OTHER INGREDIENTS WITH BEATER OR
BLENDER AND ADD TO STRAINED BEANS. POUR
INTO CRUST...BAKE 35 MINUTES.

BLACKBERRY COBBLER

COMBINE IN SAUCEPAN:

1/4 CUP SUGAR

1/4 CUP BROWN SUGAR

1/2 TBS. CORNSTARCH

1/2 CUP WATER

> BLEND WELL. COOK OVER MEDIUM HEAT, STIRRING CONSTANTLY, UNTIL THICK

> ADD: 1 TBS. LEMON JUICE AND 2 CUPS BLACKBERRIES. POUR MIXTURE INTO 2-QUART BAKING DISH.

COBBLER TOPPING:

1 CUP FLOUR

1/2 CUP SUGAR

1-1/2 TSP. BAKING POWDER

1/2 TSP. SALT

1/2 CUP MILK

1/4 CUP SOFT BUTTER

> INTO MIXING BOWL SIFT DRY INGREDIENTS AND SUGAR. ADD MILK AND BUTTER AND HEAT UNTIL SMOOTH. SPOON BATTER OVER FRUIT. BAKE AT 375 DEGREE F FOR 45 MINUTES.

CHEESE CAKE

GRAHAM CRACKER CRUST

1 8-OUNCE PACKAGE CREAM CHEESE, SOFTENED

1/2 CUP CONFECTIONER'S SUGAR

1 1-POUND, 4-1/2-OUNCE CAN CRUSED PINEAPPLE, DRAINED

1 2-OUNCE PACKAGE DREAM WHIP

WHIP CREAM CHEESE AND SUGAR UNTIL FLUFFY. STIR INTO PINEAPPLE. MIX TOPPINGS AS DIRECTED. FOLD INTO PINEAPPLE MIXTURE. SPREAD ONTO CRUST. CHILL THOROUGHLY. (TO DECORATE, RESERVE SOME OF THE GRAHAM CRACKER CRUMBS AND SPRINKLE ON TOP). STRAWBERRIES MAY BE SUBSTITUTED FOR PINEAPPLE. SERVE SIX TO EIGHT.

CHOCOLATE PIE

1 PREPARED 9-INCH (6 OZ.) GRAHAM CRACKER CRUST

1 CAN (12 FL. OZ.) NESTLE CARNATION EVAPORATED MILK

2 LARGE EGG YORKS

2 CUPS (12-OZ PKG.) NESTLE TOLL HOUSE SEMI-SWEET CHOCOLATE MORSELS

WHIPPED CREAM

WHISK TOGETHER EVAPORATED MILK AND EGG YORKS IN MEDIUM SAUCEPAN. HEAT OVER MEDIUM-LOW HEAT, STIRRING CONSTANTLY, UNTIL MIXTURE IS VERY HOT AND THICKENS SLIGHTLY, DO NOT BOIL. REMOVE FROM HEAT, STIR IN MORSELS UNTIL COMPLETELY MELTED AND MIXTURE IS SMOOTH. POUR INTO CRUST; REFRIGERATE FOR 3 HOURS OR UNTIL FIRM. TOP WITH WHIPPED CREAM BEFORE SERVING.

CUSTARD PIE

4 EGGS

1/2 CUP SUGAR

1 TEASPOON VANILLA

1/8 TEASPOON SALT

2-1/2 CUPS MILK

GROUND NUTMEG

PASTRY FOR SINGLE - CRUST PIE (SEE RECIPE ON NEXT PAGE)

FOR FILLING, IN A BOWL BEAT EGGS SLIGHTLY WITH A ROTARY BEATER OR FOLK TILL COMBINED. STIR IN SUGAR, VANILLA, AND SALT. GRADUALLY STIR IN MILK. MIX WELL. PLACE THE PARTIALLY BAKED PASTRY SHELL ON OVEN RACK. POUR THE FILLING INTO THE PASTRY SHELL. SPRINKLE WITH NUTMEG. COVER EDGE OF PIE WITH FOIL. REDUCE OVEN TEMPERATURE TO 350 DEGREES AND BAKE FOR 25 MINUTES. REMOVE FOIL. BAKE FOR 15 TO 20 MINUTES MORE OR TILL A KNIFE INSERTED NEAR THE CENTER COMES OUT CLEAN. COOL PIE ON A WIRE RACK. COVER AND CHILL TO STORE. MAKE 8 SERVINGS.

PASTRY (FOR SINGLE CRUST PIE)

1-1/4 CUPS ALL-PURPOSE FLOUR

1/4 TEASPOON SALT

1/3 CUP SHORTENING OR LARD

3 TO 4 TABLESPOONS COLD WATER

IN A MIXING BOWL STIR TOGETHER FLOUR AND SALT. CUT IN SHORTENING OR LARD TILL PIECES ARE THE SIZE OF SMALL PEAS.

SPRINKLE 1 TABLESPOON OF THE WATER OVER PART OF THE MIXTURE; GENTLY TOSS WITH A FOLK.

PUSH TO SIDE OF BOWL. REPEAT TILL ALL IS MOISTENED. FORM DOUGH INTO A BALL.

ON A LIGHTLY FLOURED SURFACE, FLATTEN DOUGH WITH HANDS. ROLL DOUGH FROM CENTER EDGES, FORMING A CIRCLE ABOUT 12 INCHES IN DIAMETER. WRAP PASTRY AROUNG ROLLING PIN. UNROLL ONTO A 9-INCH PIE PLATE. EASE PASTRY INTO PIE PLATE, BEING CAREFUL NOT TO STRETCH PASTRY.

TRIM TO 1/2 INCH BEYOND EDGE OF PIE PLATE; FOLD UNDER EXTRA PASTRY. MAKE A FLUTED, ROPE-SHAPE, OR SCALLOPED EDGE. DO NOT PRICK PASTRY. BAKE PASTRY SHELL IN A 450 DEGREE OVEN FOR 5 MINUTES.

LEMON MERINGUE PIE

1-1/2 CUPS SUGAR

3 TABLESPOONS ALL-PURPOSE FLOUR

3 TABLESPOONS CORNSTARCH

3 EGGS

2 TABLESPOONS MARGARINE OR BUTTER

1 TO 2 TEASPOONS FINELY SHREDDED LEMON PEEL

1/3 CUP LEMON JUICE

BAKED PASTRY SHELL

MERINGUE FOR PIE (SEE RECIPE ON FOLLOWING PAGE)

FOR FILLING, IN A MEDIUM SAUCEPAN COMBINE SUGAR, FLOUR, CORNSTARCH, AND DASH SALT. GRADUALLY STIR IN 1-1/2 CUPS WATER. COOK AND STIR OVER MEDIUM-HIGH HEAT TILL THICKENED AND BUBBLY. REDUCE HEAT; COOK AND STIR FOR 2 MINUTES MORE. REMOVE FROM HEAT. SEPARATE EGG YOLKS FROM WHITES; SET WHITES ASIDE FOR MERINGUE. BEAT EGG YOLKS SLIGHTLY. GRADUALLY STIR 1 CUP OF THE HOT FILLING INTO YOLKS; RETURN ALL TO SAUCEPAN. BRING TO A GENTLE BOIL. COOK AND STIR 2 MINUTES MORE. REMOVE FROM HEAT. STIR IN MARGARINE AND LEMON PEEL. GRADUALLY STIR IN LEMON JUICE,

GENTLY MIXING WELL. POUR HOT FILLING INTO BAKED PASTRY SHELL. EVENLY SPREAD MERINGUE OVER HOT FILLING, SEAL TO EDGE. BAKE IN A 350 DEGREES OVEN FOR 15 MINUTES. COOL ON A WIRE RACK. COVER AND CHILL TO STORE. MAKE 8 SERVINGS.

MERINGUE

3 EGG WHITES

1/2 TEASPOON VANILLA

1/4 TEASPOON CREAM OF TARTAR

6 TABLESPOONS SUGAR

BRING EGG WHITES TO ROOM TEMPERATURE. IN A MIXING BOWL COMBINE EGG WHITES, VANILLA, AND CREAM OF TARTAR. (SEE BELOW)

BEAT WITH AN ELECTRIC MIXER ON MEDIUM SPEED ABOUT 1 MINUTES OR TILL SOFT PEAKS FORM (TIPS CURL). GRADUALLY ADD SUGAR, 1 TABLESPOON AT A TIME, BEATING ON HIGH SPEED ABOUT 4 MINUTES MORE OR TILL MIXTURE FORMS STIFF, GLOSSY PEAKS AND SUGAR DISSOLVES. IMMEDIATELY SPREAD MERINGUE OVER PIE, CAREFULLY SEALING TO EDGE OF PASTRY TO PREVENT SHRINKAGE. BAKE AS DIRECTED IN PIE RECIPE.

PEACH COBBLER

2 CUPS FLOUR

1/2 TEASPOON SALT

PARKAY MARGARINE

4 TO 6 TABLESPOONS WATER

2 29 OZ. CAN PEACH SLICES

1 CUP BROWN SUGAR

1/2 TABLESPOON FLOUR

1/2 TEASPOON CINNAMON

1/4 TEASPOON NUTMEG

1/8 TEASPOON ALLSPICE

DASH OF SALT

1 TABLESPOON LEMON JUICE

COMBINE FLOUR AND SALT; CUT IN 2/3 CUP MARGARINE UNTIL MIXTURE RESEMBLES COARSE CRUMBS. SPRINKLE WITH WATER WHILE MIXING LIGHTLY WITH A FOLK; FORM INTO A BALL. ON LIGHTLY FLOURED SURFACE, ROLL TWO-THIRDS OF DOUGH TO 13-INCH SQUARE. PLACE IN 8-INCH SQUARE BAKING DISH. DRAIN PEACHES, RESERVING PEACH SYRUP. COMBINE SUGAR, FLOUR AND SPICES. ADD PEACHES, RESERVED SYRUP AND LEMON JUICE; MIX LIGHTLY. PLACE IN PASTRY

SHELL; DOT WITH 2 TABLESPOONS MARGARINE.
ROLL OUT REMAINING DOUGH TO A 9-INCH
SQUARE; CUT INTO EIGHT STRIPS. PLACE STRIPS
ACROSS FRUIT TO FORM LATTICE, PRESS EDGES
TO SEAL, FLUTE EDGES. BAKE AT 400 DEGREES, 40
MINUTES OR UNTIL GOLDEN BROWN.

PEACH PIE

3/4 CUP FINELY CRUSHED VANILLA WAFERS

(ABOUT 20 WAFERS)

1/2 CUP CHOPPED ALMONDS

3 TABLESPOON MARGARINE OR BUTTER, MELTED

PASTRY FOR SINGLE-CRUST PIE (SEE RECIPE, ON PREVIOUS PAGE)

2 EGGS

1 TABLESPOON LEMON JUICE

1/4 CUP SUGAR

3 16- OR 17-OUNCE CANS PEACH SLICES, DRAINED AND COARSELY CHOPPED

MIX CRUSHED WAFERS, ALMONDS, AND MARGARINE; SET ASIDE. LINE THE BOTTOM OF A PASTRY-LINED 9-INCH PIE PLATE WITH A DOUBLE THICKNESS OF FOIL. BAKE IN A 450 DEGREES OVEN FOR 5 MINUTES. REMOVE FOIL. BAKE 5 MINUTES MORE. MEANWHILE, BEAT TOGETHER EGGS AND LEMON JUICE; STIR IN SUGAR. FOLD FRUIT INTO EGG MIXTURE. TRANSFER FRUIT MIXTURE TO THE PARTIALLY BAKED PASTRY SHELL. SPRINKLE WITH WAFER MIXTURE. COVER EDGE WITH FOIL. REDUCE OVEN TEMPERATURE TO 375 DEGREES. BAKE FOR 20 MINUTES. REMOVE FOIL; BAKE FOR 15 TO 20 MORE OR TILL SET. COOL ON A WIRE RACK. COVER AND CHILL TO STORE. SERVE 8.

SWEET POTATO PIE

2 MEDIUM SWEET POTATOES

1/2 CUP BUTTER, SOFT

1 CUP SUGAR

1 TEASPOON LEMON JUICE

PINCH SALT

1 TEASPOON VANILLA

1 TEASPOON NUTMEG

1/4 CUP EVAPORATED MILK

1/4 TEASPOON ALLSPICE

2 EGGS, BEATEN

1 UNBAKED PIE SHELL

BOIL POTATOES UNTIL TENDER. PEEL; MASH AND
SIEVE THROUGH COLANDER. BEAT IN REMAINING
INGREDIENTS; MIX WELL. POUR INTO PIE SHELL.
BAKE AT 325 DEGREES FOR ONE HOUR.

POULTRY

BARBECUE CHICKEN

1 CUT-UP CHICKEN

SALT AND PEPPER

1/2 STICK MARGARINE OR BUTTER

1 BOT. OPEN PIT BARBECUE SAUCE

1/4 CUP VINEGAR

1/4 CUP PACKED BROWN SUGAR

1 CUP CHOPPED ONIONS

1 SMALL CLOVE GARLIC, MINCED

HOT SAUCE (OPTIONAL)

SPRINKLE CUT-UP CHICKEN WITH SALT AND
PEPPER. ARRANGE IN A BAKING PAN. BAKE
SLOWLY ON EACH SIDE UNTIL BROWNED AT 350
DEGREES.

MEANWHILE, FOR SAUCE, COOK ONIONS AND
GARLIC IN HOT OIL TILL TENDER IN A SAUCEPAN.
ADD ALL THE REST OF THE INGREDIENTS. SIMMER
FOR 15 MINUTES, STIRRING OCCASIONALLY. POUR
SAUCE ON BAKED CHICKEN. BAKE FOR 20 TO
30 MINUTES LONGER UNCOVERED. MAKE 4 TO 6
SERVINGS.

CHICKEN A LA KING

1/4 CUP MARGARINE OR BUTTER

1 CUP SLICED FRESH MUSHROOMS OR ONE 4-OUNCE CAN MUSHROOM STEMS AND PIECES, DRAINED

1/3 CUP ALL-PURPOSE FLOUR

1-3/4 CUPS MILK

1 CUP CHICKEN BROTH

2 CUPS CUBED COOKED CHICKEN OR TURKEY

1/4 CUP CHOPPED PIMIENTO

2 TABLESPOONS DRY SHERRY (OPTIONAL)

8 TOAST POINTS OR 4 BAKED PASTRY SHELLS

IN A SAUCEPAN MELT MARGARINE. IF USING FRESH MUSHROOMS, ADD MUSHROOMS AND COOK TILL TENDER. STIR IN FLOUR, 1/2 TEASPOON SALT, AND 1/4 TEASPOON PEPPER. ADD MILK AND CHICKEN BROTH ALL AT ONCE. COOK AND STIR TILL THICKENED AND BUBBLY. COOK AND STIR FOR 1 MINUTE MORE. ADD CANNED MUSHROOMS, IF USING. STIR IN CHICKEN OR TURKEY, PIMIENTO, AND, IF DESIRED, DRY SHERRY. HEAT THROUGH. SPOON ATOP TOAST POINTS. SERVE 4.

CHICKEN CACCIATORE

2 TO 2-1/2 POUNDS MEATY CHICKEN PIECES

(BREASTS, THIGHS, DRUMSTICKS)

1/2 CUP CHOPPED ONION

2 CLOVES GARLIC, MINCED

1 TABLESPOON COOKING OIL

1 CUP SLICED FRESH MUSHROOMS

1 8-OUNCE CAN TOMATO SAUCE

1 7-1/2-OUNCE CAN TOMATOES, CUT UP

1/2 CUP DRY WHITE WINE

1/2 CUP CHICKEN BROTH

1-1/2 TO 2 TEASPOONS DRIED BASIL, CRUSHED

1 BAY LEAF

4 TEASPOON CORNSTARCH

2 CUPS HOT COOKED FETTUCCINE

SKIN CHICKEN, IF DESIRED. RINSE AND PAT DRY.
IN A LARGE SKILLET COOK CHICKEN, ONION,
AND GARLIC IN HOT OIL ABOUT 15 MINUTES OR
TILL CHICKEN IS LIGHTLY BROWNED, TURNING TO
BROWN EVENLY. DRAIN OFF FAT. STIR TOGETHER
MUSHROOMS, TOMATO SAUCE, UNDRAINED
TOMATOES, WINE, BROTH, BASIL, BAY LEAF, 1/4

TEASPOON SALT, AND 1/4 TEASPOON PEPPER.
POUR OVER CHICKEN IN THE SKILLET. BRING TO
BOILING; REDUCE HEAT. COVER AND SIMMER FOR
30 TO 35 MINUTES OR TILL CHICKEN IS TENDER
AND NO LONGER PINK.

TRANSFER CHICKEN TO PLATTER. COVER; KEEP
WARM. DISCARD BAY LEAF. SKIM FAT FROM
TOMATO MIXTURE. STIR TOGETHER CORNSTARCH
AND 2 TABLESPOONS COLD WATER; STIR INTO
TOMATO MIXTURE. COOK AND STIR TILL BUBBLY;
COOK AND STIR 2 MINUTES MORE. SERVE OVER
CHICKEN AND NOODLES. SERVE 6

CHICKEN AND DUMPLINGS

1 2-1/2-3 POUND CHICKEN, CUT UP

1/2 CUP CHOPPED ONION

1 CUP CHOPPED CELERY

1/2 CUP CHOPPED GREEN PEPPER

2 CUBES CHICKEN BOUILLON

2-1/2 CUPS CHICKEN BROTH

1/2 TEASPOON POULTRY SEASONING

1/4 TEASPOON SALT

1/4 TEASPOON PEPPER

1 CUP WATER

DUMPLINGS (RECIPE FOLLOWS)

RINSE CHICKEN. IN A 4-1/2 QUART DUTCH OVEN COMBINE CHICKEN, CELERY, ONION, GREEN PEPPER, POULTRY SEASONING, SALT AND PEPPER. ADD CHICKEN BROTH AND WATER. BRING TO BOILING; REDUCE HEAT. COVER AND SIMMER FOR 30 MINUTES.

(DUMPLINGS ON NEXT PAGE)

DUMPLINGS

1 CAN (7.5 OZ.) BISCUITS

REMOVE BISCUITS FROM CAN AND PLACE THEM ALL TOGETHER TO ROLL OUT. ROLL OUT BISCUITS WITH A ROLLING PEN. SLICE ROLLED BISCUITS INTO A TABLESPOON SIZE.

DROP EACH TABLESPOON SIZE DUMPLING INTO CHICKEN MIXTURE. COVER, CONTINUE TO SIMMER ABOUT 40 TO 50 MINUTES OR TILL A TOOTHPICK INSERTED IN DUMPLING COMES OUT CLEAN AND THE CHICKEN IS TENDER. SERVE 4 TO 6 MAIN-SERVING.

CHICKEN JAMBALAYA

1/3 CUP CHOPPED CELERY

1/4 CHOPPED ONION

1/4 CHOPPED GREEN PEPPER

2 TABLESPOONS MARGARINE OR BUTTER

1 14 1/2-OUNCE CAN TOMATOES, CUT UP

1-1/2 CUPS CHICKEN BROTH

2/3 CUP LONG GRAIN RICE

1 TEASPOON DRIED BASIL, OR THYME, CRUSHED

1/2 TEASPOON GARLIC SALT

1/4 TEASPOON PEPPER

1/4 TO 1/2 TEASPOON BOTTLED HOT PEPPER SAUCE

1 BAY LEAF

2 CUPS CUBED COOKED CHICKEN OR TURKEY

IN A LARGE SKILLET COOK CELERY, ONION, AND GREEN PEPPER IN MARGARINE OR BUTTER TILL VEGETABLES ARE TENDER. STIR IN THE UNDRAINED TOMATOES, CHICKEN BROTH, RICE, BASIL OR THYME, GARLIC SALT, PEPPER, HOT PEPPER SAUCE, AND BAY LEAF. BRING TO BOILING; REDUCE HEAT. COVER AND SIMMER ABOUT 20 MINUTES OR TILL RICE IS TENDER. STIR IN CHICKEN; COOK TILL HEATED THROUGH. DISCARD BAY LEAF. MAKE 4 SERVINGS.

CORNISH HENS

2 GARLIC CLOVES, MINCED

2 SHALLOTS OR ONIONS, MINCED

(OPTIONAL)

1/2 TSP. FRESHLY GROUND PEPPER

1/2 TSP. SALT

1 TBSP. FRESHLY CHOPPED SAGE

(1/2 TSP. DRIED)

1 TSP. CHOPPED FRESH THYME

(1/2 TSP. DRIED)

1 CUP OLIVE OIL

2 TBSP. LEMON JUICE

1 BOX UNCLE BEN'S LONG GRAIN & WILD RICE, ORIGINAL RECIPE

6 CORNISH HENS

1-1/2 CUPS FRESH MUSHROOMS, SLICED

1/2 CUP DRY ROASTED SUNFLOWER SEEDS

PREHEAT OVEN TO 450 DEGREES F. IN A BOWL, MIX TOGETHER THE FIRST 8 INGREDIENTS AND SET ASIDE 1-1/2 TABLESPOONS OF MIXTURE. COAT THE CORNISH GAME GENS WITH THE REMAINING MIXTURE. ALLOW CORNISH GAME HENS TO MARINATE FOR 15 MINUTES. THEN BAKE AT 450

DEGREES FOR ABOUT 35 MINUTES OR UNTIL DONE AND GOLDEN BROWN. WHILE CORNISH GAME HENS ARE BAKING, COOK THE RICE ACCORDING TO PACKAGE DIRECTIONS, OMITTING THE MARGARINE AND USING THE RESERVED 1-1/2 TABLESPOONS OF MARINATE MIXTURE. WHEN THE RICE HAS COOKED FOR ABOUT 20 MINUTES, STIR IN THE MUSHROOMS, THEN RECOVER AND FINISH COOKING. STIR IN THE SUNFLOWER SEEDS WHEN RICE HAS FINISHED COOKING. SERVE ON A BED OF THE RICE, POURING A LITTLE OF THE PAN DRIPPINGS OVER THE TOP, IF DESIRED.

FRIED CHICKEN (KENTUCKY-STYLE)

3 POUNDS CHICKEN PIECES

2 (0.6-OUNCE) PACKAGES ITALIAN SALAD DRESSING MIX

3 TABLESPOONS FLOUR

2 TEASPOON SALT

2 TABLESPOONS BUTTER OR MARGARINE, SOFTENED

1/4 CUP LEMON JUICE

2 CUPS SALAD OIL

1-1/2 CUPS PANCAKE MIX

1 TEASPOON PAPRIKA

1/2 TEASPOON SAGE

1/4 TEASPOON PEPPER

1 CUP MILK

WIPE CHICKEN PIECES. COMBINE SALAD DRESSING MIX, FLOUR, SALT, BUTTER AND LEMON JUICE. COAT CHICKEN PIECES. PUT INTO A BOWL. COVER AND REFRIGERATE SEVERAL HOURS. HEAT OIL IN A LARGE SKILLET. COMBINE PANCAKE MIX, PAPRIKA, SAGE AND PEPPER. DIP CHICKEN PIECES INTO MILK, THEN PANCAKE MIXTURE. FRY UNTIL LIGHTLY BROWNED ON EACH SIDE. DRAIN. PLACE CHICKEN IN A SHALLOW PAN. SPOON REMAINING MILK

OVER PIECES AND COVER WITH FOIL. BAKE AT 350 DEGREES FOR 1 HOUR. UNCOVER AND BAKE AT 400 DEGREES FOR 10 OR MORE MINUTES. SERVE 6.

OVEN-FRIED CHICKEN (WITH "CREAM" GRAVY)

6 LGE CHICKEN THIGHS (SKIN & VISIBLE FAT REMOVED)

1 LGE CHICKEN BREAST (SKIN & VISIBLE FAT REMOVED)

LOW-FAT BUTTERMILK, AS NEEDED

1-1/2 CUPS FLOUR

1-1/2 TSPS. PAPRIKA

1-1/2 TSPS SALT

1 TSP. PEPPER

CANOLA OIL AS NEEDED

1-1/2 CUPS CHICKEN STOCK OR BROTH (FAT SKIMMED OFF)

1-1/2 CUPS EVAPORATED LOW-FAT MILK

1-1/2 TSP. MINCED GREEN PEPPER

1/4 MINCED ONION

1/4 CUP MINCED CELERY

IN A LARGE BOWL, COVER THE CHICKEN WITH BUTTERMILK. MARINATE FOR ABOUT 1 HOUR. IN A SHALLOW DISH, SUCH AS A PIE PLATE, COMBINE THE FLOUR, PAPRIKA, SALT AND PEPPER. SET ASIDE. DRAIN THE CHICKEN PIECES (DISCARDING THE MILK) BUT DO NOT PAT DRY. DREDGE THE CHICKEN IN THE SEASONED FLOUR AND SET ON A PLATTER.

HEAT A GENEROUS AMOUNT OF OIL IN A LARGE SKILLET OVER MEDIUM-HIGH HEAT. BROWN A FEW PIECES OF CHICKEN AT A TIME, ABOUT 1 MINUTE ON EACH SIDE. DO NOT CROWD THE PAN. CONTINUE COOKING IN SMALL BATCHES, THEN REMOVE THE CHICKEN TO SEVERAL LAYERS OF PAPER TOWEL TO DRAIN.

ARRANGE THE CHICKEN IN A SINGLE LAYER IN A BAKING DISH. COVER LOOSELY WITH FOIL AND BAKE AT 375 DEGREES FOR 15 MINUTES.

MEANWHILE, POUR OFF ALL THE OIL FROM THE SKILLET, LEAVING BEHIND THE BROWNED FLOUR AND ANY BROWNED BITS.

ADD THE STOCK OR BROTH TO THE PAN AND DEGLAZE (SCRAPE AND STIR TO LOOSEN BROWNED FLOUR) OVER HIGH HEAT. ADD THE EVAPORATED MILK AND VEGETABLES AND CONTINUE COOKING. IN A SMALL DISH, DISSOLVE 1 TABLESPOON OF WATER WITH THE CORNSTARCH. STIR INTO THE SAUCE AND KEEP STIRRING JUST UNTIL THE MIXTURE THICKENS SLIGHTLY. REMOVE FROM THE HEAT.

DISCARD THE FOIL FROM THE PAN OF CHICKEN AND POUR THE SAUCE AROUND THE CHICKEN. COOK 15-20 MINUTES LONGER, UNCOVERED,

UNTIL THE CHICKEN IS DONE. SPOON SOME SAUCE
OVER EACH PORTION. SERVE 6.

SWEET AND SOUR CHICKEN

1 POUND BONELESS CHICKEN BREAST

(CUT INTO CUBES)

2 TABLESPOONS OIL

1/2 CUP GREEN PEPPER STRIPS

1/2 CUP RED PEPPER STRIPS

1 CUP CARROT STRIPS

1 GARLIC CLOVE, MINCED

1 TABLESPOON CORNSTARCH

1/4 CUP SOY SAUCE

1 CAN (8 OZ.) CHUNK PINEAPPLE IN JUICE

3 TABLESPOONS VINEGAR

3 TABLESPOONS BROWN SUGAR

1/2 TEASPOON GROUND GINGER

1-1/2 CUPS ORIGINAL MINUTE RICE

BROWN CHICKEN IN HOT OIL IN LARGE SKILLET. ADD PEPPERS, CARROTS AND GARLIC; COOK AND STIR 1 TO 2 MINUTES. MIX CORNSTARCH WITH SOY SAUCE; ADD TO PAN WITH PINEAPPLE AND JUICE, VINEGAR, SUGAR AND GINGER. BRING TO A FULL BOIL.

MEANWHILE PREPARE RICE AS DIRECTED ON

PACKAGE.

SERVE CHICKEN OVER RICE. MAKE 4 SERVINGS

NOTE: MINUTE INSTANT BROWN RICE MAY BE
SUBSTITUTED FOR WHITE RICE.

TURKEY AND DRESSING

1.REMOVE TURKEY FROM BAG. SET OVEN AT 325 DEGREES.

2.FREE LEGS FROM TUCKED POSITION. DO NOT CUT BAND OF SKIN.

3.REMOVE PLASTIC BAGS CONTAINING NECK AND GIBLETS FROM THE NECK AND BODY CAVITIES. NECK AND GIBLETS MAY BE USED IN MAKING GRAVY OR STUFFING.

4.RINSE TURKEY AND DRAIN WELL.

5.IF DESIRED STUFF NECK AND BODY CAVITIES LIGHTLY.

6.RETURN LEGS TO TUCKED POSITION. NO TRUSSING NECESSARY.

7.PLACE TURKEY, BREAST SIDE UP, ON FLAT RACK IN PAN, SPRINKLE CUT UP BELL PEPPER, CELERY, AND ONIONS OVER TURKEY. BRUSH WITH MARGARINE OR BUTTER AND ROAST IN A COVERED DARK ENAMEL PAN-ROASTER COVERED.

8.ROASTING SCHEDULE:	STUFFED	UNSTUFFED
8 TO 12 LBS.	3 TO 3 1/2 HRS.	2 1/2 TO 3 HRS.
12 TO 16 LBS.	3 1/2 TO 4	3 TO 3 1/2
16 TO 20 LBS.	4 TO 4 1/2	3 1/2 TO 4

DRESSING:

1 CAN EVAPORATED MILK

1 CUP CHOPPED ONIONS

1/2 CUP MARGARINE OR BUTTER

1 PAN CORN BREAD

3 CUPS HERBAL STUFFING

2 CUPS CELERY SLICES

2 TO 2 1/2 CUPS CHICKEN BROTH

2 EGGS, BEATEN

4 TEASPOONS POULTRY SEASONING

1 TABLESPOON SAGE

SALT AND PEPPER TO TASTE

COOKED GIBLETS, CHOPPED

1 CUP CHOPPED GREEN PEPPERS

SAUTE ONIONS, CELERY, AND GREEN PEPPERS
IN MARGARINE OR BUTTER; ADD TO COMBINED
REMAINING INGREDIENTS. TOSS LIGHTLY, MIXING
WELL. PLACE IN 3-QT CASSEROLE (OR AROUND
TURKEY FOR THE LAST HOUR OR 1 1/2 HOUR);
COVER. BAKE AT 325 DEGREES F ABOUT 1 HOUR.
OR LIGHTLY STUFF DRESSING INTO BODY CAVITY
AND NECK REGION OF A 16 TO 18-LB TURKEY.

TURKEY GRAVY

PAN DRIPPINGS

TURKEY, CHICKEN OR GIBLET BROTH

1/2 CUP ALL-PURPOSE FLOUR

SALT AND PEPPER

COOKED GIBLETS, CHOPPED (OPTIONAL)

POUR DRIPPINGS FROM ROASTING PAN INTO 4-CUP MEASURE. REMOVE 1/4 CUP FAT FROM DRIPPINGS AND PLACE IN SAUCEPAN. DISCARD REMAINING FAT FROM DRIPPINGS. ADD TURKEY, CHICKEN OR GIBLET BROTH TO DRIPPINGS TO MAKE 4 CUPS. STIR FLOUR INTO FAT IN SAUCEPAN UNTIL SMOOTH. GRADUALLY BLEND IN DRIPPINGS. COOK AND STIR UNTIL GRAVY COMES TO A BOIL AND THICKENS OVER MEDIUM HEAT. CONTINUE COOKING 3 TO 5 MINUTES. SEASON WITH SALT AND PEPPER. ADD GIBLETS, IF DESIRED. MAKE 4 CUPS.

TURKEY POT PIE

2 CANS (10-3/4 OZ. EACH) CAMPBELL'S CONDENSED CREAM OF CHICKEN SOUP

2 PKG. (ABOUT 9 OZ. EACH) FROZEN MIXED VEGETABLES, THAWED

2 CUPS CUBED COOKED CHICKEN

1/2 CUP MILK

1 EGG

1 CUP BISQUICK BAKING MIX

1.PREHEAT OVEN TO 400 DEGREES F. IN 2-1/2-QT CASSEROLE MIX SOUP, VEGETABLES AND CHICKEN.

2.MIX MILK, EGG, AND BAKING MIX. POUR OVER CHICKEN MIXTURE. BAKE 35 MIN. OR UNTIL GOLDEN. SERVE 6.

SALADS

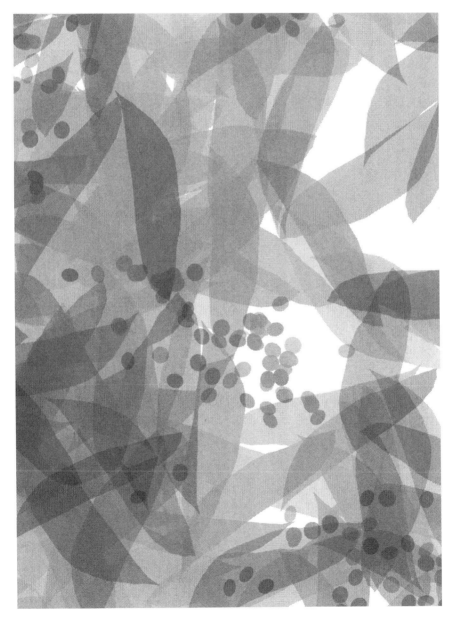

BROKEN GLASS JELLO SALAD

1-3 OZ PKG. EACH RED, GREEN & ORANGE JELLO

2-PKGS. KNOX GELATIN

1-ENVELOP DREAM WHIP

2/3 CUP POWDERED SUGAR

1 CUP PINEAPPLE JUICE

MIX EACH PACKAGE OF JELLO SEPARATELY WITH
1 1/2 CUPS OF WARM WATER. PUT EACH IN A
SHALLOW PAN. WHEN SET--CUT INTO SMALL 1 INCH
SQUARES.

MIX KNOX GELATIN WITH 1/2 CUP BOILING WATER.
MIX WELL. MIX POWDERED SUGAR & PINEAPPLE
JUICE, MIX WITH GELATIN MIXTURE.

BEAT DREAM WHIP & FOLD IN GELATIN MIXTURE &
CUT JELLO. POUR INTO ANGEL FOOD CAKE PAN--
REFRIGERATE OVER NIGHT.

CAESAR SALAD

1 EGG

1 CLOVE GARLIC, HALVED

2 TABLESPOONS OLIVE OR SALAD OIL

2 TABLESPOON LEMON OR LIME JUICE

FEW DASHES WORCESTERSHIRE SAUCE

DASH BOTTLED HOT PEPPER SAUCE

5 CUPS TORN ROMAINE

1/2 CUP CROUTONS

1/4 CUP GRATED PARMESAN CHEESE

DASH PEPPER

1 2-OUNCE CAN ANCHOVY FILLETS, DRAINED, RINSED, AND PATTED DRY

ALLOW EGG TO COME TO ROOM TEMPERATURE. TO CODDLE EGG, ADD EGG IN SHELL TO A SMALL SAUCEPAN OF BOILING WATER. REMOVE FROM HEAT, LET STAND 1 MINUTE. REMOVE EGG FROM WATER AND COOL SLIGHTLY.

CUT GARLIC CLOVE IN HALF LENGTHWISE. RUB A LARGE WOODEN SALAD BOWL WITH CUT SIDES OF THE GARLIC CLOVE. DISCARD GARLIC. ADD OIL, LEMON OR LIME JUICE, WORCESTERSHIRE SAUCE, AND HOT PEPPER SAUCE TO BOWL. BREAK THE

CODDLED EGG INTO THE BOWL. USING A FOLK OR
WIRE WHISK, BEAT TILL CREAMY. ADD ROMAINE.
TOSS TO COAT. SPRINKLE WITH CROUTONS,
PARMESAN CHEESE, AND PEPPER, TOSS TO MIX.
TOP WITH ANCHOVY FILLETS. MAKE 6 SIDE DISHES.

CHEF'S SALAD

3 CUPS TORN ICEBERG OR LEAF LETTUCE

3 CUPS TORN ROMAINE OR SPINACH

4 OUNCES FULLY COOKED HAM, CHICKEN, TURKEY, BEEF, PORK, OR LAMB, CUT INTO THIN STRIPS

1 CUP CUBED SWISS, CHEDDAR, AMERICAN OR CRUMBED BLUE CHEESE (4 OUNCES)

2 HARD-COOKED EGGS, SLICED

2 MEDIUM TOMATOES, CUT INTO WEDGES, OR 8 CHERRY TOMATOES, HALVED

1 SMALL GREEN OR SWEET RED PEPPER, CUT IN RINGS

3 GREEN ONIONS, SLICED

1 CUP CROUTONS

3/4 CUP CREAMY FRENCH DRESSING, CREAMY ITALIAN DRESSING, OR OTHER SALAD DRESSING

IN A LARGE BOWL TOSS TOGETHER LETTUCE AND ROMAINE OR SPINACH. ARRANGE MEAT OR POULTRY, CHEESE, HARD-COOKED EGGS, TOMATOES, PEPPER RINGS, AND GREEN ONIONS OVER THE GREENS. SPRINKLE WITH CROUTONS, IF DESIRED. POUR THE SALAD DRESSING OVER ALL. TOSS TO COAT. MAKE 4 MAIN-DISH SERVINGS.

CHICKEN SALAD

1-1/2 CUPS FINELY CHOPPED COOKED CHICKEN OR TURKEY

1 STALK CELERY, CHOPPED

4 GREEN ONIONS, SLICED

1 TABLESPOON LEMON JUICE

2 HARD-COOKED EGGS, CHOPPED

1/3 CUP MAYONNAISE OR SALAD DRESSING

2 TABLESPOONS SWEET PICKLE RELISH OR CHOPPED GREEN PEPPER

2 TEASPOONS PREPARED MUSTARD

3 MEDIUM TOMATOES OR LEAF LETTUCE

COMBINE CHICKEN OR TURKEY, CELERY, GREEN ONIONS, LEMON JUICE, AND 1/8 TEASPOON PEPPER. STIR IN EGGS, MAYONNAISE, PICKLE RELISH, AND MUSTARD. COVER, CHILL AT LEAST 1 HOUR. MEANWHILE, IF USING TOMATOES, CUT A THIN SLICE OFF STEM END OF EACH TOMATO. USING A SCOOP, SCOOP OUT THE CENTERS OF TOMATOES, LEAVING 1/4- TO 1/2-INCH THICK SHELLS. RESERVE PULP FOR ANOTHER USE. SERVE SALAD IN TOMATO SHELLS OR ON LETTUCE LEAVES. MAKES 4 MAIN-DISH SERVINGS.

COLESLAW

2 CUPS SHREDDED CABBAGE

1 MEDIUM CARROT, SHREDDED

1/2 SMALL GREEN OR SWEET RED PEPPER, FINELY CHOPPED

2 GREEN ONIONS, SLICED

1/2 CUP MAYONNAISE OR SALAD DRESSING

1 TABLESPOON VINEGAR

2 TEASPOONS SUGAR

1/2 TEASPOON CELERY SEED

IN A MIXING BOWL COMBINE CABBAGE, CARROT, GREEN OR SWEET RED PEPPER, AND GREEN ONIONS. FOR DRESSING, STIR TOGETHER MAYONNAISE OR SALAD DRESSING, VINEGAR, SUGAR, AND CELERY SEED. POUR THE DRESSING OVER THE CABBAGE MIXTURE; TOSS TO COAT. COVER AND CHILL FOR 1 TO 24 HOURS. MAKE 4 SIDE-DISH SERVINGS.

CRAB LOUIS

1 MEDIUM HEAD ICEBERG LETTUCE

2 6-OUNCE PACKAGES FROZEN CRABMEAT, THAWED, OR TWO 7-OUNCE CANS CRABMEAT, CHILLED, DRAINED, AND CARFILAGE REMOVED

2 LARGE TOMATOE4S, CUT INTO WEDGES

2 HARD-COOKED EGGS, CUT INTO WEDGES

LOUIS DRESSING

PAPRIKA

1 LEMON, CUT INTO WEDGES

REMOVE 4 LARGE LEAVES FROM LETTUCE HEAD. SET ASIDE. TEAR REMAINING LETTUCE INTO BITE-SIZE PIECES. ON EACH OF 4 SALAD PLATES, PLACE ONE LETTUCE LEAF. TOP WITH TORN LETTUCE. RESERVE FOUR LARGE PIECES OF CRABMEAT, TOMATOES, AND EGGS ON LETTUCE. DRIZZLE WITH LOUIS DRESSING. SPRINKLE WITH PAPRIKA. GARNISH WITH THE RESERVED CRABMEAT AND LEMON. MAKE 4 MAIN-DISH SERVINGS.

FRUIT PIZZA SALAD

1 PACKAGE (20 OZ) REFRIGERATED SUGAR COOKIE DOUGH

1 PACKAGE (8 OZ) CREAM CHEESE-SOFTENED

1/4 CUP CONFECTION SUGAR

1 CARTON COOL WHIP (THAWED)

2-3 KIKI FRUIT, PEELED AND THINLY SLICED

1-2 FIRM BANANAS, SLICED

1 CAN (11 OZ) MANDARIN ORANGES

1/2 CUP RED OR GREEN GRAPES-HALVED

1/2 CUP PINEAPPLE CHUNKS

1 JAR MARASCHINO CHERRIES

1/4 CUP SUGAR

1/4 CUP ORANGE JUICE

2 TBS. WATER

1 TBS. LEMON JUICE

1-1/2 TEASPOON CORNSTARCH

PINCH SALT

PUT COOKIE DOUGH INTO UNGREASED 14 INCH PIZZA PAN. BAKE AT 375 DEGREES FOR 10-12 MINUTES OR UNTIL BROWN. COOL.

IN MIXING BOWL, BEAT CREAM CHEESE & CONFECTIONER'S SUGAR UNTIL SMOOTH. FOLD IN

COOL WHIP. SPREAD OVER CRUST. ARRANGE FRUIT
ON TOP.

IN SAUCEPAN, BRING SUGAR, ORANGE JUICE,
WATER, LEMON JUICE, CORNSTARCH TO A BOIL,
STIRRING CONSTANTLY FOR 2 MINUTES OR UNTIL
THICKENED. COOL-BRUSH OVER FRUIT.

CHILL-STORE IN REFRIGERATOR

YIELD 16-20 SERVINGS

FRUIT SALAD

1 8-1/4-OUNCE CAN PINEAPPLE CHUNKS

1 11-OUNCE CAN MANDARIN ORANGE SECTIONS, DRAINED

1 CUP COCONUT

1 CUP TINY MARSHMALLOWS

1 8-OUNCE CARTON DAIRY SOUR CREAM

2 TABLESPOONS CHOPPED PECANS

DRAIN PINEAPPLE CHUNKS, RESERVING 1 TABLESPOON SYRUP. COMBINE PINEAPPLE CHUNKS, RESERVED SYRUP, MANDARIN ORANGE SECTIONS, COCONUT, MARSHMALLOWS, AND SOUR CREAM. COVER AND CHILL FOR 2 TO 24 HOURS. BEFORE SERVING, SPRINKLE WITH PECANS. MAKE 6 SIDE-DISH SERVINGS.

MACARONI SALAD

3/4 CUPS HELLMANN'S MAYONNAISE REAL DRESSING

2 TBSPS. CIDER VINEGAR

1 TBSP. MUSTARD

1 TSP. SUGAR

1 TSP. SALT

1/4 TSP. PEPPER

8 OZ. MUELLER'S ELBOW (ABOUT 1-3/4 CUPS) COOKED, RINSED WITH COLD WATER AND DRAINED

1 CUP SLICED CELERY

1 CUP CHOPPED RED OR GREEN PEPPERS

1/4 CUP CHOPPED ONION

1. IN MIXING BOWL COMBINE HELLMANN'S MAYONNAISE, VINEGAR, SUGAR, SALT AND PEPPER.

2. ADD REMAINING INGREDIENTS, TOSS TO COAT.

3. SEAL AND CHILL TO BLEND FLAVORS.

POTATO SALAD

4 MEDIUM POTATOES (ABOUT 1-1/4 POUND),

1/2 CUP ONIONS, CHOPPED

1/2 CUP BELL PEPPERS, CHOPPED

1/2 CUP CELERY, CHOPPED

1/2 CUP SWEET PICKLE RELISH

3/4 TSP. SALT

1/8 TSP. PEPPER

2 HARD-COOKED EGGS, CHOPPED

1 HARD-COOKED EGG, SLICED FOR GARNISH

1/4 CUP HELLMAN'S REAL MAYONNAISE

1/4 CUP MAZETTI'S COLE SLAW DRESSING

1 TBSP. MUSTARD

PAPRIKA

PARSLEY

IN A COVERED SAUCEPAN COOK POTATOES IN BOILING WATER FOR 20 TO 25 MINUTES OR TILL JUST TENDER, COOL, PEEL AND SLICE IN CHUNKS.

ADD ALL THE REST OF THE INGREDIENTS EXCEPT THE CHOPPED EGGS AND MIX. FINALLY, ADD THE 2 CHOPPED EGGS AND MIX.

TRANSFER TO A SERVING BOWL.

GARNISH WITH THE PAPRIKA, PARSLEY AND LAY
THE SLICED EGG ON TOP.

SEVEN LAYER SALAD

4-1/2 CUPS SHREDDED LETTUCE

1-10 OUNCE PACKAGE FROZEN PEAS, THAWED AND DRAINED

1 CUP THINLY SLICED RED ONIONS RINGS

2 CUPS SHREDDED CARROTS

1 CUP SALAD DRESSING OR MAYONNAISE

1-1/2 CUPS SHREDDED CHEDDAR CHEESE

6 SLICES BACON, COOKED AND CRUMBLED

LAYER LETTUCE, CARROTS, ONIONS AND PEAS IN A 2-QUART SERVING BOWL. SPREAD SALAD DRESSING OVER PEAS, SEALING TO THE EDGE OF BOWL. SPRINKLE WITH CHEESE, THEN THE CRUMBLED BACON. COVER AND CHILL SEVERAL HOURS OR OVERNIGHT. IF DESIRED, GARNISH WITH PARSLEY. PUT IN OVEN JUST LONG ENOUGH TO MELT CHEESE.

SHRIMP SALAD

1 POUND SHRIMP, COOKED, CLEANED, DICED

PINCH OF GINGER OR CURRY, TO TASTE

SALT AND FRESHLY-GROUND PEPPER, TO TASTE

1 TABLESPOON FRESH LEMON JUICE

3 GREEN ONIONS, DICED

2 RIBS CELERY, DICED

1 CUP RAW RICE, COOKED AND CHILLED

1 CUP MAYONNAISE

COMBINE SHRIMP, SEASONINGS, LEMON JUICE, ONIONS AND CELERY. FOLD INTO RICE, ADD MAYONNAISE, AND TASTE FOR SEASONINGS. IF NECESSARY, ADJUST. SERVE 4 TO 5 PEOPLE.

TACO SALADS

1 POUND GROUND BEEF

3 CLOVES GARLIC, MINCED

1 16-OUNCE CAN DARK RED KIDNEY BEANS

1 8-OUNCE JAR TACO SAUCE

2 TABLESPOON CHILI POWDER

6 CUPS TORN ICEBERG LETTUCE

4 MEDIUM TOMATOES, CHOPPED

2 CUPS SHREDDED CHEDDAR CHEESE

1 CUP CHOPPED GREEN PEPPER

1/2 CUP SLICED PITTED RIPE OLIVES

3 GREEN ONIONS, SLICED

1 MEDIUM AVOCADO, PITTED, PEELED, AND SLICED (OPTIONAL)

DAIRY SOUR CREAM (OPTIONAL)

TACO SAUCE OR SALSA (OPTIONAL)

COOK BEEF AND GARILC TILL MEAT IS NO LONGER PINK. DRAIN OFF FAT. STIR IN UNDRAINED KIDNEY BEANS, TACO SAUCE, AND CHILI POWDER. BRING TO BOILING; REDUCE HEAT. COVER; SIMMER FOR 10 MINUTES.

MEANWHILE, FOR SALADS, COMBINE LETTUCE,

TOMATOES, CHEESE, GREEN PEPPER, OLIVES,
AND GREEN ONIONS. ADD HOT MEAT MIXTURE.
TOSS TO MIX. DIVIDE AMONG TORILLA CUPS
OR INDIVIDUAL SALAD PLATES. GARNISH WITH
AVOCADO, IF DESIRED. SERVE WITH SOUR CREAM
AND ADDITIONAL TACO SAUCE OR SALSA, IF
DESIRED. MAKE 6 MAIN-DISH SERVINGS.

THREE-BEAN SALAD

1 8-OUNCE CAN CUT WAX BEANS OR ONE 8 1/2-OUNCE CAN LIMA BEANS, DRAINED

1 8-OUNCE CAN CUT GREEN BEANS, DRAINED

1 8-OUNCE CAN RED KIDNEY BEANS, DRAINED

1/2 CUP CHOPPED ONION

1/2 CUP CHOPPED GREEN PEPPER

1/2 CUP VINEGAR

1/4 CUP SALAD OIL

3 TABLESPOONS SUGAR

1 TEASPOON CELERY SEED

1 CLOVE GARLIC, MINCED

COMBINE WAX BEANS, GREEN BEANS, RED KIDNEY BEANS, ONION, AND GREEN PEPPER. FOR DRESSING, IN A SCREW-TOP JAR COMBINE VINEGAR, OIL, SUGAR, CELERY SEED, AND GARLIC. COVER AND SHAKE WELL. ADD TO VEGETABLES; STIR LIGHTLY. COVER; CHILL FOR 4 TO 24 HOURS. STIRRING OFTEN. MAKE 6 SIDE-DISH SERVINGS.

WALDORF SALAD

2 CUPS CHOPPED APPLES

1-1/2 TEASPOONS LEMON JUICE

1/4 CUP CHOPPED CELERY

1/4 CUP CHOPPED WALNUTS OR PECANS

1/4 CUP RAISINS OR SNIPPED PITTED WHOLE DATES

1/4 CUP SEEDLESS GREEN GRAPES, HALVED (OPTIONAL)

1/3 CUP WHIPPING CREAM OR 2/3 CUP FROZEN WHIPPED DESSERT TOPPING, THAWED

1/4 CUP MAYONNAISE OR SALAD DRESSING

GROUNG NUTMEG

IN A BOWL TOSS APPLE WITH LEMON JUICE. STIR IN CELERY, NUTS, RAISINS, AND, IF DESIRED, GRAPES. FOR DRESSING, IF USING WHIPPED CREAM, IN A CHILLED MIXING BOWL WHIP CREAM TO SOFT PEAKS. FOLD MAYONNAISE INTO THE WHIPPED CREAM OR DESSERT TOPPING. SPREAD DRESSING OVER THE TOP OF THE APPLE MIXTURE. SPRINKLE WITH NUTMEG. COVER AND CHILL FOR 2 TO 24 HOURS. TO SERVE, FOLD DRESSING INTO FRUIT MIXTURE. MAKE 4 TO 6 SIDE-DISH SERVINGS.

SOUPS & SAUCES

BARBECUE SAUCE

1 BOTTLE (16 OUNCES) OPEN PIT BARBECUE SAUCE

1 BOTTLE (16 OUNCES) CATSUP

3 TABLESPOONS VINEGAR

PINCH BROWN SUGAR

PINCH CHILI POWDER

HOT SAUCE TO TASTE

SEASONING SALT

COMBINE INGREDIENTS IN SAUCEPAN. BRING TO BOIL THEN SIMMER, STIRRING OCCASIONALLY, 30 MINUTES.

CHEESE SAUCE

1 TABLESPOON MARGARINE OR BUTTER

1 TABLESPOON ALL-PURPOSE FLOUR

3/4 CUP SHREDDED AMERICAN CHEESE

DASH PEPPER

3/4 CUP MILK

IN A SMALL SAUCEPAN MELT MARGARINE OR BUTTER. STIR IN FLOUR AND PEPPER. ADD MILK ALL AT ONCE. COOK AND STIR OVER MEDIUM HEAT TILL THICKENED AND BUBBLY. COOK AND STIR 1 MINUTE MORE. STIR THE SHREDDED CHEESE INTO THE COOKED SAUCE TILL MELTED. MAKE 1 CUP.

CHICKEN NOODLE SOUP

1/4 CUP (1/2 STICK) UNSALTED BUTTER

2 CUPS DICED ONIONS

1 CUP DICED CARROTS

2 CUPS DICED LEEKS

1-1/2 CUPS DICED CELERY

1/2 CUP SLICED MUSHROOMS

1/4 CUP FINELY DICED SWEET RED PEPPER OR PIMENTO

2 TEASPOONS MINCED GARLIC

3 OUNCES FETTUCINE NOODLES, IN 1-INCH PIECES

12 CUPS CHICKEN STOCK (SEE FOLLOWING RECIPE)

3 CUPS DICED CHICKEN (ABOUT 3 BREASTS)

1 TABLESPOON WORCESTERSHIRE SAUCE

2 TABLESPOONS FINELY DICED PARSLEY

SALT TO TASTE

WHITE PEPPER TO TASTE

IN A LARGE SOUP POT, MELT BUTTER OVER MEDIUM-HIGH HEAT UNTIL BUBBLING. ADD ONIONS, LEEKS, CARROTS, CELERY, MUSHROOMS AND RED PEPPER. COOK UNTIL VEGETABLES ARE WILTED, ABOUT 6-7 MINUTES, STIRRING OCCASIONALLY.

ADD GARLIC AND NOODLES AND CONTINUE TO
COOK, STIRRING FREQUENTLY, FOR 5-6 MINUTES,
OR UNTIL NOODLES ARE SLIGHTLY SAUTEED.
STIR IN STOCK AND CHICKEN, BRING TO A BOIL,
REDUCE HEAT TO MEDIUM-LOW, AND SIMMER
FOR 20-25 MINUTES, OR UNTIL CHICKEN AND
NOODLES ARE COMPLETELY COOKED. SEASON
WITH WORCESTERSHIRE SAUCE, PARSLEY, SALT AND
PEPPER, AND SERVE.

MAKE 12-14 SERVINGS

CHICKEN STOCK

4 POUNDS CHICKEN BONES

2 ONIONS WITH SKIN, QUARTERED

3 CARROTS, CUT IN 2-INCH PIECES

3 GARLIC CLOVES WITH THEIR SKIN

2 STALKS CELERY, CUT IN 2-INCH CHUCKS

2 BAY LEAVES

1/4 TEASPOON DRIED BASIL

1/4 DRIED OREGANO

1/4 TEASPOON DRIED THYME

1-1/2 TEASPOONS WHITE PEPPERCORNS

5 SPRIGS PARSLEY WITH THEIR STEMS

16 CUPS COLD WATER

PUT CHICKEN BONES, ONION, CARROTS, GARLIC, CELERY, BAY LEAVES, BASIL, OREGANO, THYME, PEPPERCORNS AND PARSLEY IN A LARGE STOCK POT AND COVER WITH WATER. BRING TO A BOIL OVER HIGH HEAT, THEN IMMEDIATELY REDUCE HEAT MEDIUM-LOW AND SIMMER FOR 1-2 HOURS (OR LONGER), SKIMMING OFF FOAM AS IT APPEARS AND ADDING WATER AS NECESSARY TO KEEP THE LEVEL CONSTANT.

STRAIN OUT BONES AND VEGETABLES AND DISCARD THEM. RETURN STOCK TO POT, RAISE HEAT TO MEDIUM, AND COOK UNTIL STOCK HAS REDUCED BY ABOUT A QUARTER, ABOUT 30 MINUTES.

MAKE 12 CUPS.

CHICKEN-VEGETABLE SOUP

4-1/2 CUPS CHICKEN BROTH (SEE RECIPE FOLLOWING CHICKEN-NOODLE SOUP)

1/2 CUP CHOPPED ONION

1/2 TEASPOON DRIED BASIL, CRUSHED

1/2 TEASPOON DRIED OREGANO, CRUSHED

1 BAY LEAF

1 10-OUNCE PACKAGE FROZEN MIXED VEGETABLES (2 CUPS)

2 CUPS CUBED, COOKED CHICKEN OR TURKEY

1 16-OUNCE CAN TOMATOES, CUT UP

IN A LARGE SAUCEPAN MIX CHICKEN BROTH, ONION, BASIL, OREGANO, BAY LEAF, AND 1/4 TEASPOON PEPPER. STIR IN VEGETABLES. BRING TO BOILING; REDUCE HEAT. COVER AND SIMMER FOR 6 TO 8 MINUTES OR TILL VEGETABLES ARE CRISP-TENDER. DISCARD BAY LEAF. STIR IN CHICKEN AND UNDRAINED TOMATOES; HEAT THROUGH. MAKE 4 TO 6 MAIN-DISH SERVINGS.

CHILI

3/4 POUND GROUND BEEF

1 CUP CHOPPED ONION

1/2 CUP CHOPPED GREEN PEPPER

2 CLOVES GARLIC, MINCED

1 16-OUNCE CAN TOMATOES, CUT UP

1 16-OUNCE CAN DARK RED KIDNEY BEANS, DRAINED

1 8-OUNCE CAN TOMATO SAUCE

2 TO 3 TEASPOONS CHILI POWDER

1/2 TEASPOON DRIED BASIL, CRUSHED

1/4 TEASPOON SALT

1/4 TEASPOON PEPPER

IN A LARGE SAUCEPAN COOK GROUND BEEF, ONION, GREEN PEPPER, AND GARLIC TILL MEAT IS BROWN. DRAIN FAT. STIR IN UNDRAINED TOMATOES, KIDNEY BEANS, TOMATO SAUCE, CHILI POWDER, BASIL, SALT, AND PEPPER. BRING TO BOILING; REDUCE HEAT. COVER; SIMMER FOR 20 MINUTES. MAKE 4 MAIN-DISH SERVINGS.

CORN CHOWDER

1 LINK POLISH SAUSAGE, SLICED IN 1/4 - INCH CIRCLES

1 16- OUNCE CAN CREAM CORN

1 10- OUNCE BOX FROZEN WHOLE KERNEL CORN

2 MEDIUM POTATOES, DICED

1 MEDIUM ONION, DICED

1 16-OUNCE CAN CHICKEN BROTH

1/4 CUP MILK

1/4 CUP BUTTER

SALT AND PEPPER TO TASTE

COMBINE ALL BUT MILK AND BUTTER IN CROCK POT. COOK
ON LOW SEVEN (OR THREE ON HIGH SETTING). WHEN
COOKED, ADD MILK AND BUTTER AND COOK ON HIGH UNTIL
HOT AGAIN.

HAM AND BEAN SOUP

1 CUP DRY NAVY BEANS

4 CUPS WATER

1 TO 1-1/2 POUNDS SMOKED PORK HOCKS OR ONE 1- TO 1-1/2 POUND MEATY HAM BONE

1-1/2 CUPS SLICED CELERY

1 CUP CHOPPED ONION

3/4 TEASPOON DRIED THYME, CRUSHED

1/2 TEASPOON SALT

1/4 TEASPOON PEPPER

1 BAY LEAF

RINSE BEANS, IN A LARGE SAUCEPAN COMBINE BEANS AND WATER. BRING TO BOILING; REDUCE HEAT. SIMMER FOR 2 MINUTES. REMOVE FROM HEAT. COVER AND LET STAND FOR 1 HOUR. (OR, SKIP BOILING WATER AND SOAK BEANS OVERNIGHT IN A COVERED PAN.) DRAIN AND RINSE BEANS. IN THE SAME PAN COMBINE BEANS, 4 CUPS FRESH WATER, PORK, CELERY, ONION, THYME, SALT, PEPPER, AND BAY LEAF. BRING TO BOILING; REDUCE HEAT. COVER, SIMMER ABOUT 1 HOUR OR TILL BEANS ARE TENDER. REMOVE MEAT. WHEN COOL ENOUGH TO HANDLE, CUT MEAT OFF BONES AND COARSELY CHOP. DISCARD

BONES AND BAY LEAF. SLIGHTLY MASH BEANS
IN SAUCEPAN. RETURN THE MEAT TO SAUCEPAN.
HEAT THROUGH. MAKE 4 MAIN-DISH SERVINGS

MINESTRONE

1/4 CUP DRY NORTHERN BEANS

1/4 CUP CHOPPED CARROT

1/4 CHOPPED CELERY

1/4 CUP CHOPPED ONION

1-1/2 TEASPOONS INSTANT BEEF BOUILLON GRANULES

1 CLOVE GARLIC, MINCED

1/2 TEASPOON DRIED BASIL, CRUSHED

1/4 TEASPOON DRIED OREGANO, CRUSHED

1/8 TEASPOON PEPPER

1 7-1/2 OUNCE CAN TOMATOES, CUT UP

1/2 CUP COARSELY CHOPPED CABBAGE

1/2 SMALL ZUCCHINI, HALVED LENGTHWISE AND SLICED (1/2 CUP)

1/2 OUNCE THIN SPAGHETTI, BROKEN (ABOUT 2 TABLESPOONS), OR 2 TABLESPOONS TINY SHELL MACARONI

2 SLICES, BACON, CRISP-COOKED, DRAINED, AND CRUMBLED

RINSE BEANS. IN A MEDIUM SAUCEPAN COMBINE BEANS AND 2-1/2 CUPS WATER. BRING TO BOILING; REDUCE HEAT. SIMMER FOR 2 MINUTES. REMOVE FROM HEAT. COVER AND LET STAND 1 HOUR. (OR, SKIP BOILING THE WATER AND SOAK BEANS OVERNIGHT IN A COVERED PAN.) DRAIN AND

RINSE BEANS.

IN THE SAME SAUCEPAN COMBINE BEANS, 2-1/2
CUPS FRESH WATER, CARROT, CELERY, ONION,
BOUILLON GRANULES, GARLIC, BASIL, OREGANO,
AND PEPPER. BRING TO BOILING; REDUCE HEAT.
COVER, SIMMER FOR 5 TO 10 MINUTES MORE OR
TILL TENDER. STIR IN BACON. IF DESIRED, SERVE
WITH GRATED PARMESAN CHEESE.

MAKE 5 SIDE-DISH SERVINGS.

MULLIGATAWNY

2-1/2 CUPS CHICKEN BROTH (SEE RECIPE FOLLOWING CHICKEN NOODLE RECIPE)

1 7-1/2-OUNCE CAN TOMATOES, CUT UP

1/2 CUP CHOPPED CELERY

1/2 CUP CHOPPED, PEELED COOKING APPLE

1/4 CUP CHOPPED CARROT

1/4 CUP CHOPPED ONION

1 TABLESPOON SNIPPED PARSLEY

1 TO 1-1/2 TEASPOONS CURRY POWDER

1 TEASPOON LEMON JUICE

1-1/2 CUPS CUBED, COOKED CHICKEN

2 CUPS HOT COOKED RICE

IN A SAUCEPAN MIX BROTH, UNDRAINED TOMATOES, CELERY, APPLE, CARROT, ONION, PARSLEY, CURRY POWDER, LEMON JUICE, AND 1/4 TEASPOON PEPPER. BRING TO BOILING; REDUCE HEAT. COVER; SIMMER 15 MINUTES, STIRRING OFTEN. STIR IN CHICKEN; HEAT THROUGH. SERVE WITH RICE AND, IF DESIRED, FLAKED COCONUT. MAKES 3 MAIN-DISH SERVINGS.

POTATO SOUP

3 MEDIUM RED POTAOTES

2 CUPS WATER

1 SMALL ONION

3 TABLESPOONS BUTTER

3 TABLESPOONS ALL-PURPOSE FLOUR

CRUSHED RED PEPPER FLAKES

GROUND BLACK PEPPER

3 CUPS MILK

1/2 TEASPOON SUGAR

1 CUP SHREDDED CHEDDAR CHEESE

1 CUP CUBED COOKED HAM

1.PEEL POTATOES AND CUT INTO 1-INCH CUBES.

2.BRING WATER TO A BOIL IN LARGE SAUCEPAN. ADD POTATOES AND COOK UNTIL TENDER. DRAIN, RESERVING LIQUID. SET ASIDE POTATOES.

MEASURE 1 CUP COOKING LIQUID, ADDING WATER, IF NECESSARY; SET ASIDE.

3.PEEL AND FINELY CHOP ONION. MELT BUTTER IN SAUCEPAN OVER MEDIUM HEAT. ADD ONION TO SAUCEPAN; COOK, STIRRING FREQUENTLY, UNTIL ONION IS TRANSLUCENT AND TENDER, BUT NOT BROWN.

4.ADD FLOUR TO SAUCEPAN; SEASON WITH PEPPER FLAKES AND BLACK PEPPER TO TASTE. COOK 3 TO 4 MINUTES.

5.GRADUALLY ADD POTATOES, RESERVED 1 CUP COOKING LIQUID, MILK AND SUGAR TO ONION MIXTURE IN SAUCEPAN; STIR WELL. ADD CHEESE AND HAM. SIMMER OVER LOW HEAT 30 MINUTES, STIRRING FREQUENTLY. STORE LEFTOVERS, COVERED, IN REFRIGERATOR.

SHRIMP DIP

5 OUNCES COOKED SMALL SALAD SHRIMP, CHOPPED (ABOUT 1 CUP)

4 OUNCES CREAM CHEESE, SOFTENED

1 TBSP. SALAD DRESSING

1 TBSP. WORCESTERSHIRE SAUCE

DASH TABASCO SAUCE (TO TASTE)

1 TSP. GRATED ONION

1 TSP. LEMON JUICE

MIX ALL INGREDIENTS. COVER AND CHILL. SERVE WITH CRACKERS, CHIPS OR VEGETABLE.

MAKE 1-1/2 CUPS.

TOMATO SOUP

2 CANS (28 OZ. EACH) CRUSHED TOMATOES

1 CAN (14-1/2 OZ.) CHICKEN BROTH

18 TO 20 FRESH BASIL LEAVES, MINCED

1 TEASPOON SUGAR

1 CUP WHIPPING CREAM

1/2 CUP BUTTER OR MARGARINE

BRING THE TOMATOES AND BROTH TO A BOIL. REDUCE HEAT, COVER AND SIMMER 10 MINUTES. ADD BASIL AND SUGAR. REDUCE HEAT TO LOW. STIR IN CREAM AND BUTTER. COOK UNTIL BUTTER IS MELTED.

VEGETABLE-BEEF SOUP

3 POUNDS BEEF SHANK CROSSCUTS

2 BAY LEAVES

1 TABLESPOON SALT

1 TEASPOON DIRED OREGANO, CRUSHED

1/2 TEASPOON DRIED MARJORAM, CRUSHED

1/4 TEASPOON PEPPER

1 10-OUNCE PACKAGE FROZEN WHOLE KERNEL CORN

2 CUPS CHOPPED, PEELED TOMATOES OR ONE 16-OUNCE CAN TOMATOES, CUT UP

1-1/2 CUPS CUBED, PEELED POTATOES

1 CUP FRESH OR LOOSE-PACK FROZEN CUT GREEN BEANS

1 CUP SLICED CARROTS

1 CUP SLICED CELERY

1/2 CUP CHOPPED ONION

IN A LARGE DUTCH OVEN OR KETTLE COMBINE MEAT, BAY LEAVES, SALT, OREGANO, MARJORAM, PEPPER, AND 8 CUPS WATER. BRING TO BOILING; REDUCE HEAT. COVER AND SIMMER FOR 2 HOURS. REMOVE MEAT. WHEN COOL ENOUGH TO HANDLE, CUT MEAT OFF BONES AND COARSELY CHOP. DISCARD BONES. STRAIN BROTH THROUGH A LARGE SIEVE OR COLANDER LINED WITH 2 LAYERS

OF CHEESECLOTH. SKIM FAT AND RETURN BROTH TO KETTLE. STIR IN MEAT, CORN, TOMATOES, POTAOTES, BEANS, CARROTS, CELERY, AND ONION. RETURN TO BOILING; REDUCE HEAT. COVER AND SIMMER ABOUT 30 MINUTES OR TILL VEGETABLES ARE CRISP-TENDER. DISCARD BAY LEAVES.

MAKE 6 MAIN-DISH SERVINGS.

VEGETABLES

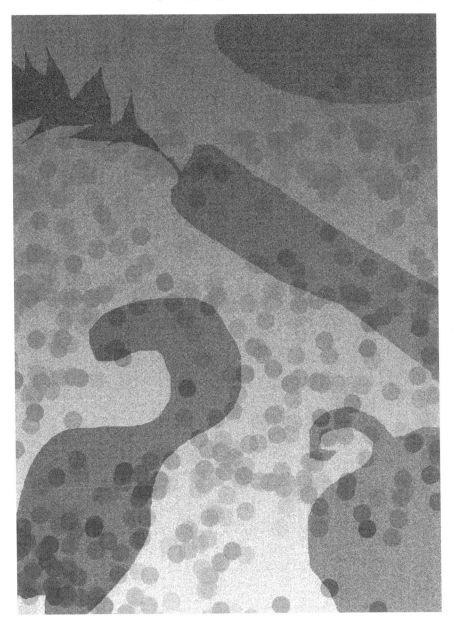

BAKED BEANS

6 CANS (16 TO 18 OUNCES EACH) PORK AND BEANS

6 SLICES BACON, CUT INTO 1-INCH PIECES

4 TABLESPOONS MINCED ONION

4 TABLESPOONS BROWN SUGAR (OR MORE TO TASTE)

4 TABLESPOONS MOLASSES

10 WHOLE CLOVES

2 TEASPOONS CINNAMON

1 TEASPOON DRY MUSTARD

2/3 CUP CATSUP

COMBINE ALL INGREDIENTS AND BAKE IN TWO 2 QUART COVERED CASSEROLE AT 350 DEGREES FOR 1 HOUR. UNCOVER AND CONTINUE TO BAKE FOR 30 MINUTES.

MAKE 22 TO 24 SERVINGS.

BROCCOLI-CARROT STIR-FRY

1/3 CUP ORANGE JUICE

1 TABLESPOON DRY SHERRY

1 TEASPOON CORNSTARCH

1 TABLESPOON COOKING OIL

1 TEASPOON GRATED GINGERROOT

1-1/2 CUPS THINLY BIAS-SLICED CARROTS

1 CUP BROCCOLI FLOWERETS

2 TABLESPOONS CHOPPED WALNUTS

FOR SAUCE, IN A BOWL STIR TOGETHER ORANGE JUICE, DRY SHERRY, AND CORNSTARCH. SET ASIDE. PREHEAT A WOK OR LARGE SKILLET OVER HIGH HEAT. ADD COOKING OIL. (ADD MORE COOKING OIL AS NECESSARY DURING COOKING.) STIR-FRY GINGERROOT IN HOT OIL FOR 15 SECONDS. ADD CARROTS AND STIR-FRY FOR 1 MINUTE. ADD BROCCOLI AND STIR-FRY FOR 3 TO 4 MINUTES OR TILL CRISP-TENDER. PUSH VEGETABLES FROM THE CENTER OF THE WOK OR SKILLET.

STIR SAUCE; ADD TO CENTER OF WOK. COOK AND STIR TILL THICKENED AND BUBBLY. COOK AND STIR FOR 1 MINUTE MORE. STIR VEGETABLES AND WALNUTS TO COAT. SERVE IMMEDIATELY.

MAKE 4 SERVINGS.

BUTTERED FRIED POTATOES

1/2 STICK BUTTER (1/4 CUP)

6 MEDIUM-SIZED POTATOES, BOILED AND DICED

1 ONION, MINCED

1/4 TEASPOON SALT

2 TABLESPOONS MINCED PARSLEY

MELT BUTTER IN FRYING PAN. ADD POTATOES AND ONION. SPRINKLE IN SALT AND PARSLEY. COOK IN A MEDIUM-HOT FRYING PAN UNTIL POTATOES BROWN ON THE BOTTOM. THEN LIFT WITH PANCAKE TURNER AND BROWN THE OTHER SIDE OF THE POTATOES.

MAKE 4 TO 6 SERVINGS.

CABBAGE

1 SMALL HEAD CABBAGE

6 STRIPS BACON

1 MEDIUM ONION, SLICED THIN

PINCH CAYENNE PEPPER

1 TABLESPOON SUGAR

SALT AND PEPPER TO TASTE

1/2 CUP GREEN PEPPER, SLICED THIN

BOILING WATER OR CHICKEN BROTH

1.REMOVE THE CORE OF THE CABBAGE AND ANY DAMAGED OUTER LEAVES. WITH A SHARP KNIFE, SHRED THE CABBAGE THIN, SET ASIDE.

2.IN A LARGE SKILLET, FRY THE BACON OVER MEDIUM HEAT UNTIL A FEW TABLESPOONS OF FAT IS RENDERED AND THE BACON IS BROWN AND CRISP. REMOVE BACON AND DRAIN ON ABSORBENT PAPER.

3.ADD THE SLICED ONION AND GREEN PEPPER TO THE FAT IN THE SKILLET AND SAUTE ABOUT 2 MINUTES. ADD THE SHREDDED CABBAGE, CAYENNE, SUGAR, SALT AND PEPPER. (IF USING BROTH, SALT AT END OF COOKING.) POUR IN ENOUGH BOILING WATER TO JUST COVER.

4.COOK AT STEADY SIMMER, UNCOVERED, UNTIL CABBAGE IS TENDER AND WATER HAS BOILED AWAY. STIR A FEW TIMES AT THE BEGINNING OF COOKING, THEN ALLOW BOTTOM TO BROWN SLIGHTLY. IF DONE BEFORE LIQUID EVAPORATES, RAISE HEAT. IF CABBAGE GETS TOO DRY, ADD MORE WATER A FEW TABLESPOONS AT A TIME. GARNISH WITH CRUMBLED RESERVED BACON.

COLLARD GREENS

ABOUT 3 POUNDS COLLARD GREENS

4 CUPS WATER

1 TO 1-1/2 POUNDS SMOKED PORK HOCKS

1 CUP CHOPPED ONION

1/2 CUP SLICED GREEN PEPPER

SALT AND PEPPER TO TASTE

1/2 TEASPOON BAKING SODA

1 TABLESPOON SUGAR

SORT YOUNG, TENDER, FRESHLY PICKED COLLARD
GREENS DISCARDING WILTED TOUGH LEAVES,
STEMS AND ROOTS. WASH GREENS THOROUGHLY.
CUT GREENS IN SMALLER PIECES.

MEANWHILE, BOIL SMOKED HOCKS IN 4 CUPS
WATER; REDUCE HEAT. SIMMER FOR 30 MINUTES.
ADD GREENS, ONION, GREEN PEPPER, BAKING
SODA, SUGAR AND SALT AND PEPPER TO TASTE.
RETURN TO BOILING; REDUCE HEAT; SIMMER FOR
ABOUT 1 HOUR OR MORE UNTIL THE GREENS ARE
TENDER AND THE SMOKED HOCK IS TENDER. MAKE
6 SIDE-DISH SERVINGS.

CREAMED CARROTS

1 POUND CARROTS, SLICED

1 TABLESPOON BUTTER OR MARGARINE

1 TABLESPOON ALL-PURPOSE FLOUR

2 TABLESPOONS FINELY CHOPPED ONION

2 TEASPOONS CHOPPED FRESH BASIL

1/2 TEASPOON SEASONED SALT

1/8 TEASPOON PEPPER

1 CUP EVAPORATED MILK

IN A LARGE SAUCEPAN, BRING 1 IN. OF WATER AND CARROTS TO A BOIL. REDUCE HEAT; COVER AND SIMMER FOR 7-9 MINUTES OR UNTIL CRISP-TENDER. MEANWHILE, IN ANOTHER SAUCEPAN, MELT BUTTER. STIR IN FLOUR, ONION, BASIL, SEASONED SALT AND PEPPER UNTIL BLENDED. GRADUALLY STIR IN MILK. BRING TO A BOIL; COOK AND STIR FOR 2 MINUTES OR UNTIL THICKENED. DRAIN CARROTS; PLACE IN A SERVING BOWL. ADD SAUCE AND STIR TO COAT.

YIELD: 4 SERVINGS

CREAMED PEAS AND NEW POTATOES

1 POUND WHOLE TINY NEW POTATOES

1-1/2 CUPS SHELLED PEAS OR LOOSE-PACK FROZEN PEAS

1/4 CUP CHOPPED ONION

1 TABLESPOON MARGARINE OR BUTTER

1 TABLESPOON ALL-PURPOSE FLOUR

1/2 TEASPOON SALT

DASH PEPPER

1 CUP MILK

SCRUB POTATOES; CUT ANY LARGE POTATOES IN HALF. IF DESIRED, REMOVE A NARROW STRIP OF PEEL FROM AROUND THE CENTER OF EACH POTATO. IN A MEDIUM SAUCEPAN COOK POTATOES IN A SMALL AMOUNT OF BOILED SALTED WATER FOR 10 MINUTES. ADD PEAS AND COOK 5 TO 10 MINUTES MORE OR TILL TENDER. DRAIN. IN A MEDIUM SAUCEPAN COOK ONION IN MARGARINE OR BUTTER TILL TENDER BUT NOT BROWN. STIR IN FLOUR, SALT, AND PEPPER. ADD MILK ALL AT ONCE. COOK AND STIR TILL THICKENED AND BUBBLY. COOK AND STIR 1 MINUTE MORE. STIR IN POTATOES AND PEAS; HEAT THROUGH. SEASON TO TASTE.

SERVE 4

FRIED CORN

REMOVE CORN FROM COB WITH SHARP KNIFE, CUTTING ONLY ABOUT HALF THE DEPTH OF THE KERNELS. WITH THE BACK OF THE KNIFE SCRAPE OUT THE REST OF THE PULP. CUT ENOUGH TO MAKE ABOUT 5 CUPS OF CUT CORN. PUT 1/3 CUP BACON FAT AND ABOUT 2 TABLESPOONS BUTTER IN A HEAVY SKILLET. HEAT FAT, ADD CORN, STIR BRISKLY FOR 1 MINUTE. ADD JUST ENOUGH WATER TO MAKE A GRAVY-LIKE MIXTURE. SEASON TO TASTE WITH SUGAR (1 TABLESPOON), SALT AND PEPPER. COOK 5 MINUTES, STIRRING CONSTANTLY. REDUCE HEAT TO VERY LOW, COVER SKILLET TIGHTLY AND SIMMER 20 MINUTES, STIRRING OCCASIONALLY. THE MIXTURE SHOULD BE THICK WHEN READY TO SERVE.

SERVE 8 TO 10.

FRIED GREEN TOMATOES

3 MEDIUM-SIZE FIRM GREEN TOMATOES

1 CUP CORNMEAL

4 TABLESPOONS UNSALTED BUTTER OR CANOLA OIL

SALT AND PEPPER TO TASTE

1/2 TEASPOON GARLIC POWDER

CUT THE TOMATOES INTO 1/2-INCH-THICK SLICES.
ADD THE GARLIC POWDER, SALT AND PEPPER TO
EACH SIDE OF THE TOMATOES. LIGHTLY COAT
THE TOMATOES WITH THE CORNMEAL. HEAT THE
UNSALTED BUTTER OR CANOLA OIL IN A SKILLET.
FRY, A FEW SLICES AT A TIME, UNTIL GOLDEN ON
BOTH SIDES, ABOUT 4 MINUTES. CONTINUE FRYING
SLICES, ADDING MORE BUTTER OR CANOLA OIL
AS NEEDED. REMOVE FROM OIL; DRAIN ON PAPER
TOWELS. SERVE 4 TO 6.

FRIED ONION RINGS

3/4 CUP ALL-PURPOSE FLOUR

2/3 CUP MILK

1 EGG

1 TABLESPOON COOKING OIL

SHORTENING OR COOKING OIL FOR DEEP-FAT FRYING

4 MEDIUM MILD YELLOW OR WHITE ONIONS, SLICED 1/4 INCH THICK

IN A BOWL COMBINE FLOUR, MILK, EGG, THE 1 TABLESPOON OIL, AND 1/4 TEASPOON SALT. BEAT WITH A ROTARY BEATER JUST TILL SMOOTH.

IN A LARGE SKILLET HEAT 1 INCH OF SHORTENING OR OIL TO 375 DEGREES. SEPARATE ONIONS INTO RINGS. USING A FORK, DIP ONION RINGS INTO BATTER, DRAIN OFF EXCESS BATTER. FRY ONION RINGS, A FEW AT A TIME, IN A SINGLE LAYER IN HOT OIL 2 TO 3 MINUTES OR TILL GOLDEN, STIRRING ONCE OR TWICE WITH A FORK TO SEPARATE RINGS. REMOVE FROM OIL; DRAIN ON PAPER TOWELS. SERVE 4 TO 6.

GARDEN-VEGETABLE STIR-FRY

1-1/2 TEASPOONS CORNSTARCH

2 TABLESPOONS SOY SAUCE

1 TABLESPOON DRY SHERRY OR ORANGE JUICE

2 TEASPOONS SUGAR

DASH PEPPER

1 CUP GREEN BEANS BIAS-SLICED INTO 1-INCH PIECES

1-1/2 CUPS CAULIFLOWER CUT INTO 1/2-INCH FLOWERETS

1 TABLESPOON COOKING OIL

1 MEDIUM ONION, CUT INTO THIN WEDGES

1/2 CUP THINLY BIAS-SLICED CARROT

1 CUP ZUCCHINI CUT INTO 1/4-INCH SLICES

TOMATO WEDGES (OPTIONAL)

FOR SAUCE, COMBINE CORNSTARCH AND 2 TABLESPOONS COLD WATER. STIR IN SOY SAUCE, SHERRY OR ORANGE JUICE, SUGAR, AND PEPPER. SET ASIDE. IN A MEDIUM SAUCEPAN COOK GREEN BEANS, COVERED, IN BOILING SALTED WATER FOR 2 MINUTES. ADD CAULIFLOWER. RETURN TO BOILING; REDUCE HEAT. COVER AND SIMMER 1 MINUTES MORE. DRAIN WELL. PREHEAT WOK OR LARGE SKILLET OVER HIGH HEAT; ADD COOKING OIL. STIR-FRY ONION AND CARROT IN HOT OIL

FOR 2 MINUTES. REMOVE FROM WOK OR SKILLET. ADD BEANS, CAULIFLOWER, AND ZUCCHINI; STIR-FRY 3 TO 4 MINUTES OR TILL VEGETABLES ARE CRISP-TENDER. PUSH VEGETABLES FROM CENTER OF WOK OR SKILLET. STIR SAUCE AND POUR INTO CENTER OF WOK. COOK AND STIR TILL THICKENED AND BUBBLY. RETURN ALL VEGETABLES TO WOK OR SKILLET. STIR VEGETABLES INTO SAUCE. COOK AND STIR 1 MINUTE MORE. IF DESIRED, GARNISH WITH TOMATO WEDGES.

MAKE 4 SERVINGS.

GREEN BEANS

1/2 POUND GREEN BEANS, WASHED AND SNAPPED

1 HAM HOCK

4 CUPS WATER

SALT AND PEPPER TO TASTE

1 TABLESPOON GARLIC POWDER

2 TABLESPOONS BACON FAT

4 POTATOES, PEELED AND SLICED INTO CHUCKS

1/2 CUP CHOPPED ONION

BOIL WATER AND HAM HOCK; REDUCE HEAT. SIMMER FOR 30 MINUTES. ADD GREEN BEANS, ONION, GARLIC POWDER, BACON GREASE, SALT AND PEPPER TO TASTE. CONTINUE TO SIMMER 20 MINUTES. ADD POTATOES AND SIMMER UNTIL GREEN BEANS AND POTATOES ARE TENDER.

HARVARD BEETS

4 MEDIUM BEETS OR 16-OUNCE CAN SLICED OR DICED BEETS

2 TABLESPOONS SUGAR

2 TABLESPOONS VINEGAR

2 TEASPOONS CORNSTARCH

1 TABLESPOON MARGARINE OR BUTTER

IN A MEDIUM SAUCEPAN COOK FRESH WHOLE BEETS, COVERED, IN BOILING WATER 40 TO 50 MINUTES OR TILL TENDER. DRAIN, RESERVING 1/3 CUP LIQUID. COOL SLIGHTLY. SLIP OFF SKINS AND SLICE OR DICE. (OR, DRAIN CANNED BEETS, RESERVING 1/3 CUP LIQUID.) IN A MEDIUM SAUCEPAN COMBINE RESERVED LIQUID, SUGAR, VINEGAR, AND CORNSTARCH. COOK AND STIR TILL THICKENED AND BUBBLY. COOK AND STIR 2 MINUTES MORE. STIR IN BEETS AND MARGARINE. HEAT THROUGH.

SERVE 4.

HONEY-GLAZED CARROTS

1 POUND CARROTS, PEELED AND SLICED

1 CUP WATER

PINCH OF SALT

1 TABLESPOON SUGAR

1 TABLESPOON HONEY

2 TABLESPOONS VEGETABLE OIL

1/2 TEASPOON GRATED LEMON RIND

COMBINE CARROTS, WATER AND SALT IN A MEDIUM SAUCEPAN. BRING TO A BOIL AND SIMMER, UNCOVERED, FOR 10 MINUTES. ADD SUGAR, HONEY AND OIL AND CONTINUE COOKING OVER MEDIUM-LOW HEAT, STIRRING OCCASIONALLY, UNTIL CARROTS ARE VERY TENDER AND LIQUID IS ABSORBED, ABOUT 15 MINUTES. WATCH SO MIXTURE DOES NOT BURN. ADD GRATED LEMON RIND AND REMOVE FROM HEAT.

SERVE 4 TO 6.

ONION ROASTED POTATOES

1 ENVELOPE LIPTON ONION RECIPE SOUP MIX

2 POUNDS ALL-PURPOSE POTATOES, CUT INTO LARGE CHUNKS

1/3 CUP OLIVE OIL OR VEGETABLE OIL

PREHEAT OVEN TO 450 DEGREES. IN A LARGE PLASTIC BAG, ADD ALL INGREDIENTS. CLOSE BAG AND SHAKE UNTIL POTATOES ARE EVENLY COATED. EMPTY POTATOES INTO SHALLOW BAKING OR ROASTING PAN; DISCARD BAG. BAKE, STIRRING OCCASIONALLY, 40 MINUTES OR UNTIL POTATOES ARE TENDER AND GOLDEN BROWN. GARNISH, IF DESIRED, WITH CHOPPED PARSLEY.

MAKES ABOUT 8 SERVINGS.

SCALLOPED POTATOES

1/4 CUP CHOPPED ONION

2 TABLESPOONS MARGARINE OR BUTTER

2 TABLESPOON ALL-PURPOSE FLOUR

1-1/4 CUPS MILK

3 MEDIUM POTATOES, PEELED AND THINLY SLICED (3 CUPS)

FOR SAUCE, COOK ONION IN MARGARINE TILL TENDER. STIR FLOUR, 1/2 TEASPOON SALT, AND 1/8 TEASPOON PEPPER. ADD MILK ALL AT ONCE. COOK AND STIR TILL THICKENED AND BUBBLY. REMOVE FROM HEAT. PLACE HALF THE SLICED POTATOES IN A GREASED 1-QUART CASSEROLE. COVER WITH HALF THE SAUCE. REPEAT LAYERS. BAKE, COVERED, IN A 350 DEGREES FOR 35 MINUTES. UNCOVER, BAKE 30 MINUTES MORE OR TILL POTATOES ARE TENDER. LET STAND 5 MINUTES. SERVE 4.

CHEESY SCALLOPED POTATOES:

PREPARE AS ABOVE, EXCEPT REDUCE SALT TO 1/4 TEASPOON. STIR 3/4 CUP SHREDDED AMERICAN CHEESE INTO THICKENED SAUCE TILL MELTED. IF DESIRED, SPRINKLE 1/4 CUP SHREDDED AMERICAN CHEESE OVER TOP BEFORE SERVING.

SQUASH AND ONIONS

2 POUNDS YELLOW SUMMER SQUASH

1/4 TEASPOON PEPPER

3 TABLESPOONS BUTTER OR MARGARINE

3 MEDIUM ONIONS (THINLY SLICED)

1/2 TEASPOON SALT

WASH SQUASH AND THINLY SLICE. MELT BUTTER IN HEAVY SAUCEPAN. ADD SQUASH, SLICED ONIONS AND SEASONINGS. COVER AND COOK FOR 20 MINUTES, OR UNTIL SQUASH AND ONIONS ARE TENDER, STIRRING FREQUENTLY. YIELD: 4 TO 5 SERVINGS. BUTTERNUT SQUASH OR ACORN SQUASH MAY BE COOKED IN A SIMILAR MANNER BUT THEY MUST BE PEELED AND THE SEEDS REMOVED.

SWEET-AND-SOUR CARROTS

3 CUPS SLICED CARROTS OR FROZEN CRINKLE-CUT CARROTS

4 GREEN ONIONS, CUT INTO 1/2-INCH PIECES

1/4 CUP UNSWEETENED PINEAPPLE JUICE

2 TABLESPOONS HONEY

2 TABLESPOONS MARGARINE OR BUTTER

1 TABLESPOON VINEGAR

1 TEASPOON CORNSTARCH

1 TEASPOON SOY SAUCE

IN A MEDIUM SAUCEPAN COOK FRESH CARROTS, COVERED, IN A SMALL AMOUNT OF BOILING WATER FOR 7 TO 9 MINUTES OR TILL CRISP-TENDER. (OR, COOK FROZEN CARROTS ACCORDING TO PACKAGE DIRECTIONS.) DRAIN; REMOVE FROM PAN. IN THE SAME SAUCEPAN COMBINE ONIONS, PINEAPPLE JUICE, HONEY, MARGARINE, VINEGAR, CORNSTARCH, AND SOY SAUCE. COOK AND STIR TILL BUBBLY. ADD CARROTS. COOK AND STIR TILL HEATED THROUGH.

MAKE 4 SERVINGS

TURNIPS & MUSTARD GREENS

ABOUT 2 POUNDS EACH OF MUSTARD & TURNIP GREENS

4 CUPS WATER

1 TO 1-1/2 POUNDS SMOKED HAM HOCKS

1 CUP CHOPPED ONION

1/2 CUP SLICED GREEN PEPPER

SALT AND PEPPER TO TASTE

1 TABLESPOON SUGAR

SORT YOUNG, TENDER, FRESHLY PICKED TURNIP AND MUSTARD GREENS. DISCARDING WILTED TOUGH LEAVES, STEMS AND ROOTS. WASH GREENS THOROUGHLY. CUT GREENS IN SMALL PIECES.

MEANWHILE, BOIL SMOKED HAM HOCKS IN 4 CUPS WATER; REDUCE HEAT; SIMMER FOR 30 MINUTES. ADD GREENS, ONION, GREEN PEPPER, SUGAR AND SALT AND PEPPER TO TASTE. RETURN TO BOILING; REDUCE HEAT; SIMMER FOR ABOUT 1 HOUR OR MORE UNTIL THE GREENS ARE TENDER AND THE SMOKED HAM HOCK IS TENDER.

MAKE 6 SIDE-DISH SERVINGS.

VEGETABLE COMBO

2 TABLESPOON WATER

1 CUP ZUCCHINI SQUASH, THINLY SLICED

1-1/4 CUPS YELLOW SQUASH, THINLY SLICED

1/2 CUP GREEN PEPPER, CUT INTO 2-INCH STRIPS

1/4 CUP CELERY, CUT INTO 2-INCH STRIPS

1/4 CUP CHOPPED ONION

1/2 TEASPOON CARAWAY SEED

1/8 TEASPOON GARLIC POWDER

1 MEDIUM TOMATO, CUT INTO 8 WEDGES

HEAT WATER IN LARGE FRYING PAN. ADD SQUASH, GREEN PEPPER, CELERY AND ONION. COVER AND COOK OVER MODERATE HEAT UNTIL VEGETABLES ARE TENDER-CRISP (ABOUT 4 MINUTES).

SPRINKLE SEASONINGS OVER VEGETABLES. TOP WITH TOMATO WEDGES. COVER AND COOK OVER LOW HEAT UNTIL TOMATO WEDGES ARE JUST HEATED (ABOUT 2 MINUTES).

MAKE 4 SERVINGS.

Made in the USA
Columbia, SC
14 December 2021